1986

Dear Kathy —

Merry Christmas!

I heard this author lecture recently and was very impressed with her message. I hope you will enjoy reading this book.

Love and all
Good Wishes

Gloria Nichols

A Woman for All Seasons

Anita Canfield

BOOKCRAFT
SALT LAKE CITY, UTAH

Library of Congress Catalog Card Number: 86-71331
ISBN 0-88494-604-5

First Printing, 1986

Printed in the United States of America

Contents

Introduction

"To every thing there is a season, and a time to every purpose under the heaven" (Ecclesiastes 3:1).

The Lord has blessed the earth with seasons to prepare, awaken, refine, and harvest new growth and more development. As it passes from season to season, every living thing on the earth moves closer and closer to its maturity.

Just as the earth experiences physical changes from time to time, so also do we experience both physical and spiritual seasons. With each passing season we move closer and closer to physical and spiritual maturity. The physical maturity is beyond our control. We are born, we grow up, and we grow older. The spiritual maturity is, however, very much in our own control. The Lord permits us to continually intervene in our own behalf.

The winter season seems to the world to be a dormant stage. This is not true, however, because if some preparation were not happening during winter, there would be no spring. Winter is a time of preparation, but it is an unseen preparation.

There is a lovely little children's story about a leaf named Freddie. The story begins in spring, when Freddie uncurls his leafy body and becomes aware of who he is. As he awakens, he becomes excited to see that he is a part of a beautiful tree. This awakening is an exciting time to Freddie and he is anxious to learn.

Then the summer comes and with it the scorching rays of the relentless sun. Freddie complains of the heat. He questions his purpose and existence: why does he have to bear all this? Then, with sudden realization, he discovers that often during the day he is shaded by his other leafy friends. And, looking down on another day, he discovers *he* is the shade to the small boys and girls, the young lovers, and the old lady—all of whom rest below him on the ground under the tree—and he is comforted.

Autumn comes and Freddie turns from bright green to a dazzling shade of red. He is astounded at this, yet another dimension of his life and his own contribution becomes even more evident. Looking around him, he sees that all the vibrant colors make for a more beautiful tree and that there is now variety in the park.

Winter takes Freddie by surprise, and he is terribly frightened as he sees his friends begin to fall one by one. "What is happening?" he cries. He hangs on in desparation, and then one day, a lone leaf, he lets go and falls softly to the ground.

Freddie looks up and suddenly sees the tree in a new perspective—it is barren, yes, but not dead, for there under the thin bark he can see tiny nodules promising yet another new leaf. This is not the end after all, Freddie thinks, but an *unseen preparation* for a new beginning! (Leo Buscaglia, *The Fall of Freddie the Leaf,* © 1982.)

The spiritual seasons of our lives come to us as the Gardener sees our need and our readiness. And our growth and maturity come as we acknowledge that Gardener and submit to his weeding and pruning.

Our spiritual winter is an unseen preparation. We don't see the growth in ourselves while we are improving. We observe winter, like Freddie the leaf, only when we look back from a different perspective. Life can be lived only forward, but it can usually best be seen backward. It is hard to see the tiny nodules of spiritual growth under the thin bark of mortality.

Our spiritual spring is a time of awakening to who we are and what we can become. It is a time of renewed self-vision and self-esteem. It is the season of catching a vision of the woman that awaits us and of rising up, never to be the same again.

The summer of our lives is a time of refinement as the scorch of trials and opposition makes us search for the shade of peace. There are times in the summer season when we become the source of shade for others, and we begin to feel an expansion of the human purpose.

The spiritual autumn brings the harvest. What good is preparation, awakening, and refinement if they do not produce good fruit? What good is the fruit if it is not harvested? And what good is a harvest if it is not shared? The autumn of our spiritual seasons brings us a more abundant harvest of purpose. We want so much to know who we really are, why we are here, what our special mission is, and how we can become all we hope and dream of becoming. What are we preparing for? What are we awakening to? Why are we being refined? Why is the harvest of ourselves and others so very important?

We are used to thinking of the answers to those questions in terms of *living* with him someday. The purpose of this book is to help us change that focus to thinking in terms of *becoming* like him some day.

It is in trying to become like Jesus that we will gain the greatest growth in self-esteem, self-vision, mission, purpose, and power. In trying to become like the Savior we can learn not just to bear afflictions, but to really become strengthened by them. In making our goal a "developmental destination," we can make this life a grand, profitable, spiritual experience.

The Savior said, "Come, follow me," and he believed many would follow him. He would not have extended such an invitation without also giving us a planting and harvesting schedule by which we might accept it.

In the pages that follow are simple, reachable ideas and goals by which we can better appreciate and use the "seasons" of our lives. In applying these principles we can know more success, more happiness, and much, much more power. The principles of growth that follow are not mine; all the credit belongs to the Gardener.

Just as it can be winter in North America and summer in South America at the same time; or just as we can have a spring thaw in winter and summer heat in autumn; or just as we can experience days of clouds mixed with bright sunshine—so are the seasons of our spiritual lives consecutive, overlapping, and simultaneous. This life is preparing, it is awakening, it is refining, and it is harvesting. We are truly women for all seasons.

Winter

An Unseen Preparation

While I was growing up in New England, I enjoyed living with four distinct seasons. My bedroom window overlooked the fields of a strawberry farm that was surrounded by forests of trees. Every winter those trees were stripped bare of foliage and stood like stern sentinels guarding the borders of the farm. The fields were covered in blankets of deep, sparkling snow. When the sun was shining, it was a crystal paradise. But when it was overcast (as most days were), it was a frozen wasteland. It was hard to imagine on those days that anything would ever be alive again.

But every spring brought a marvelous miracle. It seemed as if overnight the trees burst forth in rich green robes and the ground was covered with a thin green blanket. But that wasn't all. Along one entire side of these acres and acres of land, the farmer had planted tulip bulbs. Every spring these hundreds of gorgeous tulips burst forth from their winter's sleep and paraded their magnificent colors. It was breathtaking!

The winter months had not been a time of sleep after all, but in fact had been a time of unseen preparation. No one could see what was happening in the ground below those acres of snow that held marvels being prepared to shoot forth. Yet the preparation was really happening.

When I was first married, I met a woman with several daughters. One day while I was visiting in their home one daughter appeared at the door with a shirt for her mother to iron. A few minutes later another daughter came in and asked her mom to pick up her room. She was bringing friends over later and wanted it clean. Then a third daughter later came to make a similar request.

I mentioned to this good lady that she certainly had her work all lined up for her, and she replied to me, "I don't believe in making my children do *any* work at all. The day will come when all they'll do is work and take care of others. These years are theirs. This is their time for fun."

I thought at the time, *What a great idea! This mother really has it together!* We moved away shortly after that and I forgot all about the incident. Years later we lived in the same ward as one of those daughters. It wasn't long before I realized she had terrible housekeeping problems. One day she confided in me with a great many tears that she hated living in a pigsty—and was embarrassed—but she didn't know how to clean a house.

In this mother's enthusiasm to give her children immediate pleasure, she failed to prepare them for a fuller joy.

This lack of preparation, this lust for immediate pleasure, is a major part of what ails the world today. We are encouraged to forget preparation. "Take all you can get now, any way you can get it," we hear. Go for immediate pleasure—who cares about preparation for greater joy? The world is obsessed with immediate sensual gratification—"eat, drink, and be merry, for tomorrow we die" (2 Nephi 28:7).

The Savior has instructed us that unless we plant the seeds of preparation we cannot experience true spiritual growth. The law of the harvest says that we will reap what we sow. Seeds of success produce a garden of success. Unless we prepare to become like the Savior, we cannot become like him. Amulek taught that "this life is the time . . . to *prepare* to meet God; . . . the day of this life is the day for men to perform their labors. . . . This day of life . . . is given us to *prepare* for eternity" (Alma 34:32–33; italics added).

The winter season of our lives is mostly unseen preparation because we cannot see the results of what we have planted firmly in our hearts. We can only live life forward, but we cannot clearly see life or our real progress except when we are looking backward. The results of what we are nurturing during our season of preparation come later, in another season. But there are some seeds we can be aware of and plant and nurture as we continue in our daily growth. Such seeds can help prepare us for becoming more like the Savior.

Seeds of Success

The seeds of success are what the world calls plans. The Lord believes in preparation and plans. The world came about because of planning (see Abraham 4:21). Even the path to return to God's presence is called the "plan of salvation." What does that tell us? That there were a few planning sessions, no doubt.

A television program about the Air Force Survival School reminded me of my dad's adventure stories of when he went through that same survival course. The objective was to teach a soldier how to keep alive if he should be shot down or lost, and how to escape if he should be taken captive.

On this television program it was shown that the men in training did something wrong. They had been sloppy in their execution of the instructor's orders. In real life they would have been killed. The instructor shouted, "Do it right in drill, and you'll do it right in real life."

Part of my family's preparedness is to have periodic fire drills. We've mapped out an escape plan, and every so often we climb in our beds and Steve sets off the smoke detector. We have practiced until we can follow the plan perfectly. We believe that if we do it right in drill, we'll do it right in real life.

When Neil Armstrong walked on the moon, the world remembered his famous words, "One small step for man, one giant leap for mankind." But few people remember what he said later: "It's beautiful, just like we planned it, *just like drill!*"

The seeds of success are called plans. In all the human soul there is only one place suitable for planting such important seeds; it is in the "fleshy tables of the heart" (2 Corinthians 3:3). That small piece of flesh has been fertilized and made ready for such seeds by a Gardener who understands clearly the roots that will strengthen our souls.

But we must not make small plans, we must make big plans. President Spencer W. Kimball said: "Make no small plans. They have no magic to stir men's souls" (quoted in Ardeth G. Kapp, *Blueprints for Living*, vol. 1 [Provo, Utah: BYU Press, 1980], p. 78).

I know someone who made small plans. She was married in the temple and knew what would happen if she became unfaithful. She knew what it would do to her family and children. She thought of excommunication, possible divorce, or at least separation. She pondered the shame, the embarrassment.

Yet she still made a small plan to have a few moments of what she assumed would be great pleasure. It wasn't. She realized she had risked everything she *really* wanted in life—and for a mess of pottage.

She's coming back, thanks to the great plan and program of repentance it includes. Her plans are changing, and they are bigger than they've ever been.

There are others I know who have big plans:

—A young eighteen-year-old woman in Mississippi has big plans for a temple marriage. If that doesn't come, she says she'll not settle for less.

—There are no small plans for two lady missionaries in San Bernardino who both interrupted successful careers, one in physics and the other in business, to go on a mission.

—Big plans for a recent Brigham Young University graduate include a mission, temple marriage, master's degree, children, and eventually another mission. She just left for Ecuador to begin fulfilling her dreams.

—A mother of six in San Antonio who just completed her first year of college (it took her four years) has big plans to graduate when her youngest does.

—A good friend in Las Vegas took some craft ideas and labored over a drawing board to create patterns. Her big plans include a national market.

—A sister in New York who can't have any children adopted one, and now she has big plans to adopt many more, regardless of their color or health.

—A grandmother in Idaho has big plans for politics. She's an assemblywoman now. What's next? Senator? Governor?

—A twelve-year-old girl in Denver has big plans to read the standard works by the time she's eighteen.

—A woman in Canada doing genealogy for her English ancestors has big plans to save money for a trip to the homeground in England.

—An Australian sister who gathers her nonmember neighbors once a week and gives them family home evening lessons has big plans to help convert many.

—A sister in Salt Lake City plans big by entering the Pillsbury Bake-off each year, writes books, and inspires others.

—A mother of eight sons has big plans as she guides them toward Eagle Scouts, Duty to God awards, missions, and temple marriages.

—A twenty-five-year-old convert in Japan has big plans that include the conversion of family, friends, and loved ones to Jesus Christ.

—A sister in South Africa lives her big plans as she strives to be an example of accepting all God's children as equals.

Do you think Camilla Kimball married a future prophet because she made small plans to get married—or because she made big plans to marry a righteous man?

Do you think Sharlene Wells was Miss America because she made small plans to get by on her looks, or because she made big plans to develop her talent and intellect as well?

Do you think Paula Hawkins is a U.S. Senator for Florida because she made small plans to go out and vote, or because she made big plans to be involved in fighting for justice and truth?

Do you think Lee Provancha Day became an acclaimed ballerina because she made small plans to take a few dance lessons, or because she made big plans to practice and learn to dance well?

By and large, we create our own opportunities. No one should ever depend on luck to bring success in any endeavor. The reason why some understand this concept and others don't lies in their preparation; it lies in making plans and planting the seeds of success. It was not opportunity that brought this world about, it was planning. It was not luck that brought us to this world; it was our planning to come. And we will not return to our Father in Heaven just because we get lucky; those who return will have planned and prepared for such an opportunity.

Even if unexpected opportunities occasionally come our way, we can only take advantage of those opportunities if we are aware of their true potential and are prepared to act accordingly. The one-third that rebelled in the council in heaven will never be able to say that they didn't have the opportunity to come here. They had the opportunity, but they did not take advantage of it. They had not prepared properly, so they chose to follow Lucifer instead.

We all choose to make things happen. Eventually everything that we do involves making a choice.

Now, find a piece of paper. Right now. Take out a pencil and make some plans. Start simple: maybe make one plan for improving your spirituality, one for a talent, one for a relationship (husband, child, relative), one for interactions with your fellowmen, and one for your physical self.

Try it. Write down five simple plans. Set a date by each one indicating *when* you want to accomplish it. Then plan *how* you will do it and *who* can help you.

Do something to implement this plan each day—or each week. Get a notebook, record your progress, and review it often. It really works. If you follow this simple process you'll find you can accomplish far more than if you never wrote down a plan.

Our ultimate plan should be to become like the Savior. But unless we *plan* for that, it won't happen.

Sometimes our plans don't turn out as we wanted them to. We hold on to hopes and dreams, but find one day that things aren't turning out the way we planned.

What then? Do we give up? Do we quit dreaming and planning? Has God forsaken us?

Remember the song "Climb Ev'ry Mountain"? It counsels: "ford every stream, follow every rainbow, till you find your dream," and I'd like to add, "or until you find an alternative dream." Sometimes when you get to that dream or that plan, even that alternative plan, you do indeed discover it's "a dream that will take all the love you can give." We should always keep *planning!*

I have a friend who had planned to be an Olympic ski champion. But the summer before the Winter Olympics she had an accident that left her paralyzed from the waist down.

Suddenly things weren't turning out the way she had planned, and her life seemed plunged into despair and darkness. But my little friend is not easily discouraged, and she decided to get back up and climb another mountain. She made an alternative big plan. She went to college and became a psychologist, and today she does vocational (and inspirational) counseling for other crippled and paralyzed people. And indeed, she's confided, this is a dream that's taking *all* the love she can give.

The families of Günter Wetzel and Peter Strelzyk of East Germany had a big plan that took all the love they could give. Theirs were big plans for freedom.

They wanted freedom more than anything else. They smelled it, breathed it, dreamed it, and ached for it until they could no longer stand it. They decided they must escape to West Germany.

They made desperate attempts to build, engineer, and fly a hot air balloon that would carry the eight of them to freedom. Failure followed failure, including a late night attempt in which they almost made it, but instead landed in the perilous "border zone" area on the east side. They made bigger plans—and a bigger balloon. Theirs is a story of man's indomitable will to succeed! (You can see this story in the Walt Disney movie *Night Crossing* or read it in Jürgen Petschull, "The Great Balloon Escape," *Reader's Digest*, March 1980, pp. 107–13.)

Equally inspiring is the story of Robert and Jona Hutyra of Czechoslovakia. Somehow they obtained a bootleg copy of the *Reader's Digest* that contained the story of the Wetzel and Strelzyk families. Robert spent several months painstakingly translating every word of English into his native tongue. As he and his wife read the story over and over again, they too tasted freedom on their lips, breathed it in their nostrils, and knew they must try—or die! And so, buying and scrounging small pieces of fabric, they worked for over two years making a hot air balloon, working secretly late into the nights. And they, too, knew of a dream that was taking all the love they could give as they encountered problem after problem. But that night of freedom came; they boarded their homemade craft and sailed away in the black night —away to freedom and much, much bigger and better plans! (Jeff Davidson, "Above the Clouds to Freedom," *Reader's Digest*, July 1984, pp. 38–44.)

Plan to become like the Savior. It is a big plan, but it is an attainable one. He invited us to do it, to "become even as I" (3 Nephi 12:48).

We will accomplish this not in one giant effort but in planning our days and lives so as to be obedient to the gospel laws. We can become like the Savior if we prepare for a royal harvest instead of just a bushel of fruit.

"We are half-hearted creatures, fooling around with drink and ambition, when infinite joy is offered us; like an ignorant child who wants to go on making mud pies in the slums because he cannot imagine what is meant by an offer of a holiday by the sea." (C.S. Lewis, *A Mind*

Awake [New York: Harcourt, Brace and World, 1968], p. 168.)

Seeds of Power

Nearly everyone wants to be in charge of her life, to have the inner power to take charge and move forward, and to make life happen for her.

When we look into the lives of those whom we admire for having such power, we rarely find a life free from burdens and problems. In fact, we often regard others as "take-charge people" *because* of their problems, not in spite of them. We see the difference between the weak person and the one with inner power by observing how each handles his problems.

Don't run away from your problems. Don't lie in bed with the sheets pulled over your head. Meet your problems head on!

Probably we make at least one million decisions in our lifetime. We have a feeling of hopelessness when we cannot isolate and identify problems or know what is wrong. Even if we can identify problems, we feel hopeless when we don't know how to conquer them.

Elder Marvin J. Ashton illustrates what Satan would want us to believe about our setbacks and problems:

My thoughts have turned back to a bewildered and confused young man in a huge city. He had lost his way. In desperation he stopped a man on the sidewalk and said, "How do I get to such-and-such a destination from here?" After considerable thought, with the skyscrapers, dense traffic, confusing streets, winding rivers, freeways, bridges, tunnels, and so on in mind, the man said, "You can't get there from here." (*Ensign,* December 1971, p. 99.)

Often we may feel lost and don't know how to get "there" from where we are at the moment. We have all had that feeling at some time. As Elder Ashton points out, this is exactly what Satan wants us to feel. This feeling is so immobilizing that we feel defeated before we even attempt to solve a problem.

If we carefully plant the seeds of power, seeds of decision making, we can become excellent problem solvers and decision makers in a relatively short period of time. As these seeds germinate and the roots take hold, we can find strength in our own brains and abilities. With that strength we can reach to the light we need for greater growth, the light of the Holy Ghost. We will be able to move ourselves further and further through the winter darkness into the warmth of other seasons yet coming to nourish us.

We can see clearly that in becoming like the Savior we must also become "as gods, knowing good and evil" (Moses 4:11). We will learn this only through experiencing opposites, through making choices and solving problems.

Let's discuss some suggestions that can help you, in five minutes, to become an excellent problem solver and decision maker.

1. *Identify the problem.* Isolate it—filter the facts. You need to analyze yourself, the facts, and those people involved. If you study it out, somewhere in the process will come the information. It might take a little practice at first, but recognizing a problem requires studying and analyzing the facts.

2. *Search out all the laws that apply.* Everything is governed by laws—earthly laws, spiritual laws, gospel laws, worldly laws. What laws apply to your problem?

3. *Understand the alternatives and consequences.* List

the alternatives to the problem and under each one list the pros and cons. I am always amazed at how many people don't know how to do this. For example:

Exercising

PRO	CON
I will live longer.	It takes time.
I will be in better shape.	It may require equipment
I will be more attractive.	that I don't have.
	I don't know where to
	start.

You need to know which course will improve the situation better, and which course will make it worse. Now, this is where most people get stopped. Satan works hardest here. If he can keep you vacillating, like a pendulum, he has succeeded in stopping your progress. The times in my life when I have been frozen in indecision have been when I've been the weakest, the most immobilized, and certainly the least productive. You *must* go on from here to the next step!

4. *Make a decision.* Most of our daily decisions will not decide our eternal destination. Many of these can be made quickly. In such a matter, the next step is to choose a course of action. After you have weighed out everything (pros and cons) and studied all the laws that apply, logically choose the best alternative. Now, this is the important consideration: *it frequently doesn't matter if you make the right or the wrong decision at this point* (that is, as long as your decision does not break any moral laws and truly is the best alternative); *what matters most is that you make a decision.* When you stand undecided, you stand uncommitted and vulnerable to every threatening blow Satan will deal you. Even if you make a wrong decision, some-

where down the road is often a place to bail out or change your direction. Practice making decisions on less important matters so that you can develop the confidence you will need to face more important issues.

Major decisions that are affected by our values and life-styles may demand a more thoughtful approach to ensure that we don't make a mistake. You may need to proceed cautiously as you begin to formulate your decision, and you may find yourself repeating some parts of this decision-making process several times to ensure that you are doing what is right for you. This does not mean that you continually reevaluate and never act on your decision. Rather, as you begin the journey on which this decision will take you, you will want to look at your map often. Make sure you are still going in the direction you want to go. If so, proceed. If not, rethink your decision.

5. *Confirm that decision.* You don't have to wander blindly into decisions that are life-changing. The Lord wants to help us and he will. He said:

> But, behold, I say unto you, that you must study it out in your mind; then you must ask me if it be right, and if it is right I will cause that your bosom shall burn within you; therefore, you shall feel that it is right.
>
> But if it be not right you shall have no such feelings, but you shall have a stupor of thought that shall cause you to forget the thing which is wrong; therefore, you cannot write that which is sacred save it be given you from me. (D&C 9:8–9.)

After you've made a significant decision, the Lord wants you to come to him and ask if it's the right decision. He is not going to make the decision. Many times he has impressed me with this thought, *I gave you a brain, now use it!* We need to learn to ask the *right* questions.

Not "What do you think I should do?" but rather "This seems to me to be what I ought to do. Is it right?"

What if no answer comes? Then we should proceed with that decision. Perhaps the Lord wants us to use our brains more; perhaps other teaching lessons are coming. Again, if it proves to be wrong, in many cases we can regroup and bail out!

6. *Give the decision your full effort!* Never make a decision without committing to it. Take a teaspoon and start shoveling away at the mountain!

Now, let's apply these six steps to some problems.

You've had your house up for sale for two years. There has been no buyer in all this time. You have moved to another city and have had renters in the house. There is damage. The renters are moving out and you either have to rent the house again or move back—or something. Paying for two houses is draining you.

1. Identify the problem.
    You can't sell your house.
2. What are the laws that apply?
    Financially you are responsible.
    It is a major negative cash flow.
3. List alternatives and consequences.
    You could let the house go into foreclosure, but
       that would ruin your credit.
    You can get another renter and hope for less
       damage.
    You could move back.
    You could leave it vacant.
    You could reduce the price for a quicker sale.
4. Make a decision.
    Choose the best alternative you can with the information you have.
5. Ask the Lord to confirm it. If no answer comes,
    proceed with your original decision.

6. Continue in your effort to make your choice work out.

Now let's look at a not so obvious problem:

A woman at church appears to be rude to you. You think she's being sarcastic, but you're not sure. You feel uncomfortable around her. What can you do?

1. Identify the problem:

    You feel uncomfortable around this lady. You aren't sure whether she likes you. *You* are the one who feels uncomfortable. As you filter the facts you might ask yourself:

    > Did I have any contact with her in which I might have offended her?

    > Have I unintentionally ignored her?

    > Do I feel threatened by her?

    > Does she remind me of someone who intimidated me? (Like my seventh grade Physical Education teacher!)

2. What are the laws that apply?

    She is not responsible for your attitude toward her, *you* are.

    She can't make you feel uncomfortable—only you can allow that to happen to yourself.

    If indeed she doesn't like you, you *must* forgive her if you want to progress yourself.

    The gospel teaches us patience with each other.

3. What are the alternatives?

    You might go to her and ask if anything is wrong.

    You could ignore the whole thing and pretend everything is okay.

    You could be rude to her or let her know what you think.

    Make a list of each alternative and write the pros and cons. Study them.

4. *Make* a decision.

Choose the best solution. Maybe it will even be a combination of choices.

5. *Pray.*

Ask the Lord to confirm your choices and ask for the Spirit to be with you and guide you. Ask for a sweet spirit.

6. Give it the effort.

Do the part you have control over. In this situation you have control only over yourself. What if, after all this, you find out it's true—she doesn't like you? You've tried to be loving and include her, but she continues in her behaviors. What then?

Not every problem has an immediate solution. Another part of *effort* is to endure with faith until a solution comes or the problem is resolved.

It would be much easier if decisions were always a clear-cut choice between good and evil, but they are not. Most often our decision will be a choice between *several* good alternatives, if not between good and bad ones.

We can take courage at the first recorded earthly decision. It was made by a woman. She had to choose between multiplying the earth and not eating of the tree of knowledge of good and evil. She couldn't keep both commandments; that much she understood.

She didn't have all the facts, all the understanding; she didn't have the whole picture, but neither do we when we make most of our decisions.

I believe, however, that she weighed some alternatives because of the *true* part of Satan's temptation, "ye shall be as gods, knowing good and evil." She chose the alternative with the greatest good, and our contrast of opposites began.

It is only through opposites, through choices and problems, that we can become "as gods, knowing good and evil" (Moses 4:11). We will become more like the

Savior as we take charge of more and more of our own life and become more masterful in our choices between good and evil.

Seeds of Knowledge

Knowledge is the new frontier. Thomas Wolfe wrote: "If a man has a talent and cannot use it, he has failed. If he has a talent and uses only half of it, he has partly failed. If he has a talent and learns somehow to use the whole of it, he has gloriously succeeded, and won a satisfaction and a triumph few men ever know!" (John Bartlett, *Bartlett's Familiar Quotations* [Boston: Little, Brown, & Co., 1980], p. 1049.)

One of my favorite scenes in any movie is the one from *Auntie Mame* in which Mame is standing on the stairway and bellows, "Life is a banquet and most . . . fools are starving to death!"

Why did you buy this book? Why do you buy any book?

The purpose of educating ourselves is to (1) increase our ability to think more deeply, (2) develop competence in skills, (3) heighten new interests, (4) understand ourselves better, and (5) add more meaning to old principles.

Isn't this why you bought this book? Isn't that why you buy any book, or take any class, or any mini-class? Read what Belle Spafford said on her eighty-first birthday when one of her children asked her what she had learned in all her years.

> She replied: "During the four-score and one years of my life, I have learned that earth life is short; that time is extremely valuable and should not be dissipated; that the teachings of the Church are sound and reasonable and true; that obedience brings sure rewards; that disobedience brings naught but sorrow.

"I have learned that adversity is the common lot of everyone. Life's testing lies in whether or not one is able to overcome and rise above it. I have learned that family ties are sacred. No effort is too great to safeguard them. . . . I have learned that freedom is a priceless heritage. Government of the people, by the people, and for the people must not be allowed to perish from the earth. These things I know of a certainty.

"I have learned that the inborn natures of male and female differ. This is the supreme law of God. The interests of both are best served when respect is shown for this law." (Shirley W. Thomas, "Women of Charity: Belle S. Spafford and Barbara B. Smith," *A Woman's Choices: The Relief Society Legacy Lectures* [Salt Lake City: Deseret Book Company, 1984], p. 15.)

Sister Spafford planted seeds of knowledge that prepared her for a harvest of greatness in herself and in others. The words she spoke sound simple, as if they were common knowledge, but few people in this world have a testimony or the knowledge of the things of which Sister Spafford spoke.

The Lord had a word to say about education and a desire to learn: "Seek ye diligently and teach one another words of wisdom; yea, seek ye out of the best books words of wisdom; seek learning" (D&C 88:118).

Simple advice—the counsel of the Lord is always simple to understand when we comprehend by the Spirit. Learning is meant to revitalize the vision of our potential, and the potential of those we may influence.

President Joseph F. Smith asserted:

I . . . admonish the Latter-day Saints everywhere to cease loitering away their precious time, to cease from all idleness. . . .

Converse upon subjects that will be of interest to your associates, and at your social gatherings . . . seek out of the best books knowledge and understanding. Read history. Read philosophy, if you wish. Read anything that is good, that will elevate the mind and will add to your stock of knowledge, and that those who associate with you may feel an interest in your pursuit of knowledge and of wisdom. (*Gospel Doctrine* [Salt Lake City: Deseret Book Company, 1939], p. 235.)

Read great books. Rub shoulders with great characters. Stretch your imagination. Experience new ideas.

Can you read? No, I don't mean vocalize or interpret words and print. Can you read in a way that causes you to *ponder* and *wander in thoughts,* deep, deep thoughts of your own?

Somerset Maugham said that he believed not many learn to do this. Those who do, he believes, are the ones who are heard from. He said:

You see people who think they are reading. They sit and look at the print in some bulky, flabby Sunday paper for an hour, for three hours perhaps, or at some cheap magazine, or at some flashy paperback novel. You see people looking at that sort of thing for hours. They merely want something to lean their feeble minds upon to save them from the effort of thinking. This is not reading.

Read books not to gain information. You can get that, cut and dried, in the encyclopedia. Read not to get ideas, but mainly to gain intellectual and moral stimulus. Read in this mood and the great books will increasingly enable you to think out your own ideas. One soon tires of a book that does not make him feel now and then like getting up and walking the floor under the impulse of some larger vision of truth.

In a great library, you get into society in the widest sense possible, for in these silent gatherings . . . the highest is at the service of the lowest, with a grand humility. . . . In a library you become a true citizen of the world. ("A Confidential Question," reprinted from *Wisdom* in *National Education Association Journal,* April 1965, p. 19.)

Might I suggest a few things that might help you to read and to feel more mental creativity from your reading.

First, don't go overboard. Start with *one* book. How many times have we all come home from the bookstore or library loaded down with many books and then not finish even one? We become discouraged, and we often quit before we even start. Buy *one* good book that interests you. It could be one of the classics you've never read, or one by a prophet or General Authority, or one from a well-loved philosopher or scholar. Make reading that book your goal. Don't worry about the unread volumes that await you. Concentrate on your one book as a goal for today.

Second, don't think you have to finish a book just because you bought it, or because it is loved and accepted by everyone else. I have wasted much time in my life trying to finish books that either I wasn't ready for or whose authors I didn't feel a kinship with.

For example, years ago I had heard about Anne Morrow Lindbergh's *Gift from the Sea* and borrowed a friend's copy to read. I hated it! At that time in my life my thoughts weren't random-abstract, and I lived very much on the surface. I wasn't ready for her book yet. Years later when a friend gave it to me as a gift, I opened it, began reading, and this time devoured and feasted on every word. Life's experiences had brought me to a place in which I could relate with Mrs. Lindbergh's analogies. The book became a place where I could walk in deep, deep thoughts of my own.

Take another popular book, one written by a well-known author. This book was a gift to me several years ago, and I was excited to read it because so much public approval had been given it. When I was around chapter three I closed the book and thought, *maybe I'm not ready for this yet, either.* A year or two went by and I tried to read it again. Again, I was only a few chapters into the book when I became bored and found I was not relating. About two years ago I tried again, this time closing it after a few pages. It was clear to me then that what the author was saying was what I believed, but his expression was too concrete-sequential for my random-abstract way of viewing things.

We are all different and unique, and no one author is going to reach or relate to everyone in terms of personality. That is one reason I keep talking about "cherishing our differences," because we need them all. All those differences make up the great power called influence. So somewhere out there are books with personalities that will not only inspire you but will also cause you to wander in deep, deep thoughts of your own. Don't waste time reading a book because everyone else says it's great. Read what you can relate to and what inspires you.

Third, get rid of clutter activities. There is so much "clutter" time in a day. We need to unlayer ourselves by first unlayering our environment. My sister said she started with her kitchen. Out went all those gadgets she bought because she thought that *someday* she would use them. Then her unfinished project closet went to Deseret

Industries. Anything that she hadn't touched in two years and that always left her feeling guilty when she came across it was sent to Deseret Industries.

We spend countless hours each month in clutter activities that need to be eliminated, just as my sister's gadgets were, so we can have time to really read. Certain television shows, unnecessary phone visiting, extra time spent wandering in a mall, reading too much newspaper material—all these and other activities you know of clutter your life. No one needs to tell you what they are. Replace some of these activities with a few pages "out of the best books" and see if your mind doesn't transcend to a higher level of understanding and learning.

Victor Hugo wrote in his classic masterpiece *Les Miserables:* "If there is anything more poignant than a body agonizing for want of bread, it is a soul which is dying of hunger for light" (*Les Miserables* [New York: The Modern Library, n.d.], p. 842).

God is *not* still learning. He is all knowing. Our quest is to become like him. We have more than just the capacity to do that, we have an inborn spiritual inclination to seek that perfection.

That desire is truly verified to us as we hear the stories about the American prisoners of war in Vietnam. Under their horrible confinements, and deliberately deprived of all reading material, they pooled their memories and their imaginations. Their resources became unbelievable and unending. As they opened a few doors, they discovered this led to many more doors (ideas).

Together they remembered hundreds of verses of scripture and hundreds of songs. They got to know each other's dreams and goals even better than their own families knew them. In their minds they built houses, remodeled garages and basements, restored old buildings, and invented hundreds of ideas for making money, saving time, and organizing space. They played mental games of golf, tennis, and basketball over and over, and when they returned home many found they had actually improved their game in that way. They mentally took trips and recorded every detail: the food, scenery, people, and points of interest. They taught each other classes, everything from aerodynamics to woodworking to pancake making.

All of these things were done from memory and with no materials or tools. And the exciting part is this: they *really learned*.

The desire to learn is an integral part of our spiritual selves.

Seeds of Self-Control

The seeds of self-control lie in learning to act and not react. In trying to become like Jesus we can see into his life and understand how he *acted* and not *reacted*. Even when he was personally assaulted, he never allowed himself to retaliate.

There is no one more unhappy than the person who continually reacts. Such people are always subject to others' moods. A woman who only reacts finds her emotional center not within herself where it should be, but rather in the world outside of her. Whatever the emotional level is around her, she finds herself being raised and lowered by it. She falsely believes she is out of control and cannot stop the process. She doesn't know why she is so miserable.

Every criticism, cross word, and real or imagined snub plunges the reactor into depression. Every confrontation or squabble with family or children pushes the reactor to higher levels of verbal violence. The faintest suggestion of unpopularity clenches the reactor into bitterness.

Peace within ourselves can't be achieved until we master our own actions and determine our own attitudes —until we learn to act and not to react. We must not let other people determine whether we will be happy or sad, rude or courteous, hateful or loving, successful or unsuccessful.

The only true control is self-control. And self-control is all we can truly and ultimately hope to possess. The only true possession is self-possession, or, in other words, self-mastery.

This is *why* we are here—to master ourselves. We are trying to become like Jesus, trying to become Christlike. Now or later, if we want the celestial kingdom, we are going to have to learn to conduct our lives according to the inherited godlike attributes in us. Becoming Christlike is learning to *act* on truth and true principles instead of throwing away our self-control and allowing ourselves to react to what goes on around us.

Some reactors solve problems by getting drunk, some curse God, some become bitter, some react openly to the faults of others by judging and criticizing them, some are sarcastic, and some leave the Church. I know a couple who reacted to a humble mistake of the bishop by saying, "We'll never set foot in that church until that bishop is released!" Despite his apologies, this couple reacted, and even though other bishops have come and gone, they are still inactive.

Here is the key to know if you are acting or reacting:

If you are acting, you *intelligently decide* what is the right and wrong thing to do. You are able to think it through for a few moments, and you try to take positive action. This is all accompanied by feelings of peace, order, and self-esteem.

If you are reacting, the clear-cut line between right and wrong is missing; you become confused and mixed up.

You cannot tell if your response is right or reactionary. You feel you don't know how to handle your problems. This is all accompanied by feelings of anger, frustration, confusion, and low self-esteem.

One day I had to go to the bank to sign some important papers. I had made an appointment to sign the papers, which was good because I was "running" that day and didn't have time to sit around while the correct people were notified and the papers were located. When I approached the clerk, who mistakenly had not been told of my appointment, she was curt and abrasive with me. I tried to explain the papers and the need to find them that moment. She became even more abrasive, and I made a sarcastic remark and turned on my heel and left. As the revolving door swung me to the outside, a little voice said, "Now, Anita, you're not going to get away with that!" I found myself in front of her desk apologizing. She sheepishly extended her hand and also apologized. She had been frustrated with a day of mismanagement and irate customers. She went and found my papers and we parted good friends.

Learning how to act and not react is easier said than done. I know; I've been a reactor and still am sometimes, but there are some things I'd like to share with you that have really helped me.

1. Take time to assess the situation or source before you speak or react. If you give yourself *one minute,* it can make *hours* of difference, hours of success. This takes real self-control. If at first you don't feel confident in removing yourself *mentally* from the situation then leave *physically* for a moment or two (even three). Walk away, go in another room, lock yourself in the bathroom, go for a drive.

Take time to seek the spirit of discernment. Pay attention to your feelings: are you confused or peaceful?

The spirit of contention comes from Satan. Take time to recognize his hostility and confusing influence on you. "He that hath the spirit of contention is not of me, but is of the devil, who is the father of contention, and he *stirreth up the hearts*" (3 Nephi 11:29; italics added).

Take time to seek the spirit of love and discernment, the Holy Ghost. Don't let your heart be stirred up. Removing yourself for a few moments can save hours of struggling to get the Spirit back.

Don't lower yourself to a devil level! We were meant to seek a higher level. Lehi said to his son Jacob: "There is a God, and he hath created all things, . . . *things to act and things to be acted upon* (2 Nephi 2:14; italics added). And in verse 26, Lehi makes sure Jacob understands that of all God's creations men are to "act for themselves and not to be acted upon."

Each wrong choice we freely make, makes us less free and more acted upon. There was a group of young Latter-day Saints that had two choices—to act or react. They were out in the Arizona desert around Phoenix on a youth outing when one of the girls was bitten by a rattle-snake. Now their choices were to administer first aid and get the girl to a hospital or to chase and kill the rattle-snake. They had plenty of time to do either one, but not enough time to do both. They chose to chase the snake. They found it, beat it, and it died. Unfortunately, several days later, their friend lost her leg below the knee. They had failed to take their *one minute of peace* and it caused them hours of grief. (See H. Burke Peterson, *Ensign*, Nov. 1983, p. 59.)

When our environment injects venoms, we can sit down quickly, assess the situation, open the wound, and draw out the poison before it does any damage to us. Or we can pursue the hostile thing and quickly become immobilized, right where Satan wants us.

2. Use the action dialogue. If you want to be a person of action and not reaction, you first have to know the action words. They are *ask, seek, knock, pray, love, work, believe*. The reaction words are *hate, anger, revenge, lust, fear, doubt, strife*. Let's use the action words as they apply to learning to act.

Ask for help, for forgiveness.
Seek the Holy Ghost, the spirit of discernment.
Knock looking for solutions; try to help others.
Pray and draw closer to God; seek his counsel.
Love and forgive others; look past their faults; serve.
Work to give more effort for self-control.
Believe having faith in yourself, others, and God; appreciate your differences; and have patience with yourself.

Now let's try some action dialogue:
"I forgive you."
"I love you."
"I'm sorry you feel that way, but what you are saying isn't true."
"What may I do to help you feel better?"
"Let me see if I understand what you are saying or what you mean."
"Help me to understand what you mean."
"Is this the best way?"
"Can we start over?"

3. Ask yourself an important question: How will I feel one hour from now? So many times I've wallowed in misery only to discover that an hour or so later I had to pull myself out of it because no one else would.

One day I received a phone call conveying very depressing news. By the time I hung up and got to the top stairs I was discouraged. Lying down on my bed I wanted to moan away the afternoon, but the thought came,

"Anita, how will you feel an hour from now?" It was three-thirty. In an hour I knew I'd have to get up and around, make dinner, and go on with the night's activities. I knew that eventually before the night was over I would have to pull myself together and press on. If I could do it in an hour or so, why not *now*, I thought. Why waste the hour? We eventually end up having to rely on cheerfulness, so why not decide to rely on it at the onset of our problems and save ourselves unnecessary anguish?

4. Last, but not least, we should ask ourselves, "What would Jesus do?" Don't ask what you would do if he were here, but what *he* would do. In that sixty-second break, that one minute of collecting thoughts, this question has made me take the time to reflect on similar situations in his life, or qualities he showed in his life, and has helped me gain a perspective of the moment.

The following story illustrates how one person's *actions* changed a negative situation.

> I sat on a San Francisco bus going home, tired and depressed after one of those days when nothing seemed to go quite right. It was rush hour, and the bus was packed with people—dull-eyed, tired, aching, and short-tempered.
>
> A large, package-laden lady got on the bus. Every seat was taken, so she had to stand in the aisle near me. *War horse,* I thought as I looked at her drawn and bitter face. That was a pretty good description.
>
> Seated across the aisle next to her was a small, plain-looking lady, someone you wouldn't ordinarily notice. She looked up at "War Horse" and her face was lit with a smile. "Could I hold your packages?" she asked. "It's so hard to stand when your arms are full."
>
> The woman glowered in confusion and looked

away. But when she looked back, the smile was still there. Her wrinkled brow eased some as she handed over the packages. "They *are* very heavy," she said. "There are two pairs of specially made shoes for my crippled son, and they weigh twenty pounds a pair." She paused, and the next words seemed very hard for her to say: "Thank you." They chatted on, and as they did, she smiled. Her whole face softened and her body relaxed.

Soon the seated lady got off and the other woman sat down in her place. But her expression had changed, and she smiled up at the young coed standing above her. "Could I hold your books for you? It's difficult to hold on with books sliding every which way."

The girl smiled back, and as she gave up her books I heard her ask, "Did I hear you say you have a son who goes to Jefferson? That's where I go to school."

I had to get off at the next stop, but I imagined that smile traveling all over San Francisco. I too smiled, and wasn't so tired anymore." (Jane Bunker Newcomb, "The Traveling Smile," *Ensign,* Aug. 1985, p. 67.)

Learning to act and not react requires patience and practice. It comes, slowly maybe at first, but with each success comes inspired new courage. I promise you that if you try these simple ideas, you will see a real change come into your life and feel great success in action and increased self-esteem.

I noticed as soon as I opened the door
that the fellow was surly, and so
with a frown just as black as the one that he wore
I angrily told him to go.

Now I hadn't the slightest intention to be
as surely, uncivil and hateful as he,
but that was the trick that he played upon me.

Another chap came to my doorstep that day,
and a twinkle he had in his eye.
With a smile on his face he began in a way
that prompted a gentle reply.
Though a stranger he was, I was eager to be
as gracious, good-natured, and kindly as he,
and that was the trick that he played upon me.

Since those visits I've thought in this life that we live
and the lesson seems simple to learn:
We get back a smile for the smile that we give
and a frown brings a frown in return.
If I chuckle, with chuckles I'll surely be met.
Just as I set my lips, so all lips will be set.
And that is a trick that I mustn't forget.
(Edgar A. Guest, "The Trick," *Favorite Poems Old and New,* [Syracuse: Century Company, 1928], p. 604.)

Seeds of Love

Greet the day with love in your heart. Plant seeds of love that will produce good fruit. I remember one year that gave me some of the hardest days in my life. Don't misunderstand me; I did not say the worst days, but rather the *hardest* days. In truth they were also some of the *greatest* days of my life because in my extremities I came to an even greater witness that God lives, and I have learned more.

Elder Neal A. Maxwell writes:

One of the dimensions of worshiping a living God is to know that he is alive and living, . . . not a retired God whose best years are past . . . whom we worship

36

for what he has already done. . . . He is, . . . at once, in the dimension of the past, . . . the present and the future, while we labor constrained by the limitations of time. . . . Time can tug at us and play so many tricks upon us if we lack eternal perspective. (*Things as They Really Are* [Salt Lake City: Deseret Book Company, 1980], p. 29–30.)

Eternal perspective—we must develop it if life's episodes are to have meaning. True eternal perspective helps us see the purpose in all of life and it helps us to deal with what may seem to be very dark days.

Winston Churchill, in an address to the boys of Harrow School on 29 October 1941, said:

Do not let us speak of darker days; let us speak rather of sterner days. These are not dark days: these are great days—the greatest days our country has ever lived; and we must all thank God that we have been allowed, each of us, . . . to play a part in making these days memorable. . . . (Bartlett, *Familiar Quotations*, p. 745.)

What inspiring words! These *are* great days, sisters.

In all the days of mortal life these are the greatest days thus far. Never have our own personal lives been potentially closer to becoming like God. In the premortal existence we weren't as much like God as we are today. We had no physical bodies, we had no mortal experience from which to solidly know good from evil and the results of such choices, and we could not exercise faith as we can here.

While certain peoples have attained great spiritual heights (such as the city of Enoch or those described in 4 Nephi 1:1–18), we truly live in the dispensation of the *fulness of times*. These are great days for God's children.

In all of history these are in many ways the *greatest* days. There are more resources available, more talent and creativity, more inventions, more conveniences, more comforts, more luxuries, more free time, more miracles, more scientific marvels, more feats of medicine, and more choices available to us.

The gospel is rolling forth as the stone cut from the mountain. There are more missionaries, more scriptures, more direct contact with leaders and members, more compassionate service, more money to work with, more temples, more wards, more stakes, more chapels, more resources, more programs, and more of the most righteous men and women that have ever been born.

We have only to remember that Abraham could not find ten righteous men in Sodom (Genesis 18:23–33) or that Noah and his family spent a year in the ark, while the rest of the inhabitants of the world drowned because of their unrighteousness (Genesis 18:11–19:14). Do we remember Moroni, John, the three Nephites, and others who roamed this earth lonely in their righteous lives?

These *are* great days!

May I suggest ten little steps to help you greet each day with love in your heart. They work; they sound simple, but the reality of joy in your life can be simple, by following the gospel of Jesus Christ.

1. Get a motto to live by. Sister Camilla Kimball's motto is Never Withhold a Generous Thought. President Kimball's was Do It. Mine is This Is As Good As It Gets. Some may think my motto suggests resignation, as if to say, "Ah well, there's nothing I can do; I might as well give up." No! No! That is not the case.

This Is As Good As It Gets is meant to inspire me to search for new meaning and to have joy from today no matter what the day brings. It is my personal reminder of why I'm here, a reminder of eternal perspective. "Why complain, Anita? This is what you came for. Don't wait for happiness; this is as good as it gets. Make your happiness *now*, a part of each day!''

I have a couple of other mottos: Nothing Ventured, Nothing Gained, and Rise Up and Never Be the Same Again.

Little thoughts help us greet and work through each day. They are little tools to dig away the weeds of despair. Let me challenge you to right now take out a piece of paper and to write a motto to live by. Write down some words that will inspire you to greet each day with love in your heart.

2. You can greet each day with more love in your heart by deciding the night before that you will love another day on earth. Then kneel down and *ask* the Lord for it.

3. In the morning, tell the Lord, ''Good morning, I'm thankful you answered my prayer. I'm glad to be alive today. It's good to have another day to work out my salvation.''

4. Smile first thing when you wake up, and don't stop there. Smile at yourself in the mirror, and smile at everyone you see and meet, especially your family. It is staggering to me to see the effect my smile (or lack of it) has on my family in the morning and on others throughout the day. Smile, even if your heart is aching. It makes a difference.

5. Hum a pretty song, or sing a note or two. Again, the soft notes of music can change your attitude and the attitude of those around you. Also, if you play some lively or beautiful music in the morning, you will notice a *big* difference.

6. Answer the phone with enthusiasm. Answer cheerfully. It is distressing to others to hear a sickly ''hello'' on the other end, and it only makes you feel worse about yourself. Your weak ''hello'' will probably cause your caller to hang up sooner than he would have otherwise.

Often after you act negatively you punish yourself, saying "Why did I act like that?" Be enthusiastic!

7. Say "please" and "thank you." Be courteous to others and watch the response. Your day will be more filled with love as you show love through words and even written notes. Watch faces light up and watch how others begin to thank you.

8. Find a role model and emulate her. What is a role model? It's not a Linda Evans or a Joan Collins; most of us don't have their packaging anyway. A role model is someone who has been faced with the same ordinary choices you have, who perhaps has been down some of the same roads you have, and is happy and making her days successful. Look into her life and see what she's doing—ordinary things—that you might also do to find more success and happiness.

9. Don't deliver your problems everywhere. How many times have we solicited every listening ear to unload our problems on? There is no need to discuss problems except with those directly involved in solving them. If we do, people shun us, thinking, *Oh no, here comes Sue with that long face and story again.* No one really cares to hear about our day-to-day struggles, except perhaps the Lord. It's not that we aren't loved. It's just that everyone else has day-to-day struggles too.

10. Repeat your motto aloud at the beginning *and* at the end of the day. My good friend has a motto: I Am Going Home. She repeats this motto three times a day. She'll make it. Her saying is not just a motto; it has become a goal.

Seeds of Self-Esteem

Self-esteem is our own responsibility. As we experience our winter seasons of preparation it is important that we plant seeds of self-esteem. Those seeds are the ability to recognize the difference between insecure and secure thoughts, the difference between positive and negative thoughts. Insecure thoughts are those that defeat and discourage us, and secure thoughts are those that inspire and encourage us. When you are confronted with confusing thoughts, ask yourself this question, "Am I inspired by this or am I feeling defeated?" If the answer is negative, you must recognize it as an insecure thought and take action. That action often means weeding and tilling the soil of your mind and replanting it with good thoughts.

Years of thoughts—do's and don'ts, family chatter, ideas, gossip, children's stories, conversation, classroom discussions, beliefs, criticisms, praise—have brought us to where we find ourselves today.

These thoughts started out like flimsy cobwebs and have become like unbreakable steel cables that either strengthen or shackle our characters.

> Therefore, sanctify yourselves that your *minds* become single to God, and the days will come that you shall see him. . . . Remember the great and last promise which I have made unto you; cast away your *idle thoughts* (D&C 88:68–69; italics added.)

Thinking is mostly talking to yourself. We talk to ourselves 70 percent of the time we are awake. It is what we think, conditioned by years of *saying* what we think, that makes us feel and believe what we are.

I have a friend who was told for years that she was unlovable, unteachable, and just no good. She went to college and told everyone she was unlovable and unteachable. She felt and believed this was true until she realized she had to accept responsibility for her own thoughts (and her own self-esteem). She decided that others could say this about her, but she didn't have to accept it. She began to dwell on her good qualities and soon discovered she was lovable, teachable, and worth a great deal. Today she has become a leader of women.

If we think positive, good, great thoughts and then *say* those thoughts for years, we will feel and believe we are good, great, positive people. If, however, we think bad, ugly, negative thoughts and say them for years, we come to believe we are ugly and worthless. We are what we think and say.

If you plant strawberries, what do you get? If you plant tomatoes, what do you get? If you plant spinach, what do you get? That's right; you get what you plant.

What do you get if you "plant" these thoughts?

—I am dumb.

—I am ugly.

—I am a bad mother.

—I am unhappy.

—I am untalented.

Negative thinking is a habit. Like any habit it requires time, practice, and patience to change negative into positive thinking. It can be done. Of that I *know* personally. The method is simple but not always easy.

Habit is one of those "soft" words. *Habit*—it doesn't sound like such a bad thing, does it? Just try changing a bad one! What are the chains of hell? They are habits! Satan would bind us down with the chains of our habits, and that includes our habits of thought.

There is a concept known in the world as the "I am" concept. It says simply that we can change our negative thoughts to positive ones by choosing to affirm to ourselves, I am positive, good, lovely, and many other good things.

Look at that list of negatives again in a new light:

Negative	Change to Positive
I am dumb.	I am intelligent, I have the Holy Ghost, and I am the offspring of God.
I am ugly.	I am lovely, created after the image of God.
I am a bad mother.	I am a good mother; motherhood is an attitude; I have the desire to bear and nurture children.
I am unhappy.	I am happy; I can count my blessings and see the Lord's goodness in my life.
I am untalented.	I am talented; the Lord has given everyone at least one gift (D&C 46:11–12).

If you planted those positive thoughts what would you get? That's right! After practice and saying it, you would begin to believe it and become that person. "As [she] thinketh in [her] heart, so is [she]" (Proverbs 23:7).

In becoming like the Savior we are to take upon ourselves his name. *Christ* means *anointed one.* When we take on his name we are calling ourselves one who is anointed to someday become as God and inherit all that he has.

Jesus is another name for the premortal Jehovah. The LDS Bible Dictionary tells us that *Jehovah* denotes "the eternal I AM," the term by which Jehovah identified himself to Moses (Exodus 3:14). So we can say that to us *Jesus* denotes I AM. These two words are the first person singular of the verb "to be," and with our doctrine of eternal progression we can readily think from "to be" to "to become"—to become like God.

Expand the I AM even more and see how the double meaning retestifies over and over that Jesus is the Son of God, and that we may be one, "even one in me as *I am* one in the Father" (D&C 35:2; italics added).

And then our own *secure* thoughts can be enlightened as we see our relationship with the Savior develop when *we take on his name* and work to become like him:

> I AM a child of God.
> I AM a daughter of God.
> I AM trying to be like Jesus.
> I AM—Anita.

Satan wants to immobilize us, and one way he can do that is through our own negative thoughts. He has the power to bruise our heels. His power is terrible because it immobilizes us almost immediately. But we have the greater power—to crush his head. It is the power of free agency, the power of positive thoughts, the power of I AM!

Making this power work requires effort. A steam engine won't work unless there's a fire; a car won't start without the key. Learning thought replacement is a good key. In a lesson I taught on bad thoughts versus pure thoughts I demonstrated thought replacement with a cardboard tube and wads of black paper and white paper. Filling the tube with black wads, I explained that they were insecure, negative thoughts; by shoving a white wad in, I made a black one fall out. Little by little the white (secure) thoughts replaced all the black ones. That is exactly how it works in our minds. We have to force the bad ones out by putting good ones in.

We do this by dwelling on a positive experience of the past, by an I AM affirmation, by repeating our motto, by concentrating on a good quality, or by picturing ourselves as we want to be.

I have a friend who comes from a family of educated people. School was important in their home life as they were growing up. All were fine students, except one brother who was nearly failing school. One year he got a teacher who understood this power of picturing. When his first report came it was marked with straight A's. Knowing it was a mistake, the boy went to see the teacher, who said, "Oh no, you are a straight A student, you just don't know it yet. I thought you should see what your report card should be like." That was a remarkable moment for this young boy. He now could *see* himself as a straight A student, and ultimately he became one. Today he is a prominent heart surgeon.

There is another great story of thought replacement and picturing.

Many years ago, I failed in a business venture. My cash was gone and I was behind in my rent. My family was not getting proper food. My first thought, of course, was to get a job, but this turned out to be more difficult than I had anticipated. Other businesses were also folding.

Things went from bad to worse. I ran the gamut from feeling sorry for myself to trying to reaffirm my faith in myself. I tried to mix with successful people and attended inspirational lectures to try to keep my confidence up.

I called on one business firm after another in an effort to obtain a job. When I was refused, I left with bitterness. Then I got to the point of not actually expecting to be hired. This attitude got the natural results. I became short-tempered with my family; in short—I became a regular heel.

Then one day as I was driving home after one more defeat with a prospective employer, I stopped at a crosswalk to let a youngster pass. I raced my engine in anger for he was intolerably slow. Then I looked at him. This was no ordinary boy. He wore a grey and blue baseball suit. He carried a bat on his shoulder and onto the bat was laced a glove. I could see the outline of a baseball in his pocket. He wore his baseball cap at a jaunty angle. He was every inch a big-league baseball player.

Tears welled in my eyes as he slowly crossed the street. The boy was terribly clubfooted and could hardly drag his body across the walk. He smiled and waved me on, but I did not smile back at him. I just sat there, feeling terribly ashamed, until a horn in back of me bade me go forward. This little fellow, struggling across the street, had envisioned himself as a great baseball player. He had the greatest of hope. He *was* a baseball player. I silently said a prayer for the boy and drove on.

The next day, I found a job and began enjoying myself in the work I know best. The sight of that happy crippled boy had, when I was finally ready, transformed me into a man." (Albert R. Johnson, *Success Unlimited* [W. Clement Stone PMA Communications, Inc.], June 1970.)

Seeds of Persistence

Last, but not least, when we hit a snag in our unseen preparation, and we will, we must plant seeds of persistence.

We go along, we make some progress, we take four steps forward, and then we falter, slip, and fall twelve steps backward!

We set goals and ideals with enthusiasm, but when we

experience failure or fatigue we give up. And then we feel worthless.

I love this sentence I heard a few years ago: "Our ideals should be stars to steer by, not sticks to beat ourselves with." The filmmaker and producer Kieth Merrill won an Academy Award for Best Documentary with his film *The Great American Cowboy.* He wrote:

> When I decided to do the film *The Great American Cowboy,* I was sitting in my office, warm and comfortable. I said, "I think I will do a film about rodeo cowboys." All of a sudden I found myself standing in the bucking chutes. The goal was no longer white, clean, and beautiful. Bucking chutes tend to make your shoes messy. You will find that somewhere between setting and reaching a goal, you'll end up in the muck and mire of the arena of life. That's when you have to increase your persistence. Don't change the goal. Don't say, "The goal wasn't good because I have manure on my boots." Don't say, "I must not be capable of reaching that goal." Say, "I've got to work harder, try harder, get up earlier, study harder, go to church more, pray harder, follow the principles of the gospel." Be persistent. Then you will reach those goals and find yourself becoming the person you imagine yourself to be. (Kieth Merrill, "Deciding About Decisions," *The Time of Your Life: Selections from the New Era Magazine* [Salt Lake City: Bookcraft, 1977], p. 11.)

There is no mystery to persistence; it is *will power,* the will to do. It is not a negative "hanging on by sheer force." Persistence is so much more than that. It is an active (action) will to do.

There are some ways we can keep our ideals from

getting out of hand and thus becoming sticks to beat ourselves with. Here are ten ideas that keep our goals up in the sky as stars to steer by.

1. Select goals and ideals that apply to us as individuals. Don't worry that you don't seem to "fit in" to what others around you feel is important. (I am speaking of individual goals, of course, and not those things that have to do with the Savior's plan of salvation.) Don't compare yourself to others. You sisters who are divorced, widowed, single, or mothers are individuals first. Don't worry what the lady across the street is doing; set your goals as they apply to you.

2. Do high priority work first. Start each day with a list of things to be done *in order of priority.* Don't put off a high priority just because it's a big job—do it now! The freedom and relief are worth the extra effort.

3. Build up a love for accomplishment. The easiest way to do this is to outline two or three small things you want to accomplish. Make a goal to get one done a day. The thrill you feel at seeing your work finished is unbelievable. Now, add a more difficult goal and go on from there.

4. Try new things. This also fosters a love for accomplishment. Don't get in a rut; don't cook the same things every week; don't wear the same colors every day; don't do the same thing every weekend. Variety is the spice of life. Besides, if you don't try new things, you'll never know what other talents you have. I was afraid to make crepes, but decided to try it. I loved it and learned all I could. Today it is one of my family's most enjoyable things to eat.

5. Go the extra mile. It isn't at all crowded. You will find that if you do a little (not even a lot) more than what is required, you'll be accomplishing and succeeding at a faster rate than you ever dreamed possible. My husband

and I discovered that by paying only one hundred dollars more a month on a real estate loan we would cut the total interest payments by more than half and have the property paid for in less than half the time. Going the extra mile brings ten times the rewards of the first mile.

6. Work hard to overcome obstacles that might weaken your efforts. Satan will work harder on you as you work harder for self-mastery and accomplishment. Remember all the principles and keys we discussed in this chapter and apply them harder and longer when the obstacles come. After the battle of Waterloo, some of the British boasted, "We were braver than the French." To this the Duke of Wellington replied, "No, we weren't; we were only brave five minutes longer." Be brave five minutes longer than the obstacle.

7. Become a yes-no person. Don't be wishy-washy. Remember the previous comments on decision making. Learn to be a good problem solver and decision maker. Remember, there's always an alternative.

8. Always expect the unexpected. There is only one thing constant about life—it is constantly changing. The other day I told my husband, "Things haven't turned out the way I planned them when I was twenty-one." He said, "What have you done about it?" And I answered, "I keep regrouping!" Sisters, plan to keep regrouping. This is what we came here for. This is as good as it gets.

9. Keep getting up. Elder Paul H. Dunn has said; "It's not how many times you fall that counts, it's how many times you pick yourself back up!" A ski instructor told me once, "If you're not falling, you're not learning." How true of life!

10. Desire to do the will of the Lord. I love the persistence of Nephi: "*I will go and do* the things which the Lord hath commanded, for I know that the Lord giveth no commandment unto the children of men, save he shall

prepare a way for them that they may accomplish the thing which he commandeth them.'' (1 Nephi 3:7; italics added.)

And I love the Savior's example of persistence to do the will of his Father. He wanted out of his great ordeal if at all possible, but then he said, "Not my will, but thine be done" (Luke 22:42).

Sisters, we have discussed the winter of our lives, the mostly unseen preparation of life. Life can best be understood backward, but it can be lived only forward.

Preparation is exciting and securing. "If ye are prepared ye shall not fear" (D&C 38:30). Jean Taylor is a woman who added to her years of unseen preparation more preparation, and today she is a confident, self-sufficient woman.

Happily ever after. Yes, that was how I had planned my life—to live happily ever after being a supportive wife and a loving mother. And at age 31, happily ever after seemed to me a reality. Just seven months earlier, I had given birth to our fourth son. My husband, at age 33, after serving as the elders quorum president, as the second counselor in the bishopric, and as a member of the high council, had just been sustained as the bishop of our ward. And now we were on our way to Salt Lake to attend April conference, with happily ever after in our grasp. But then that car came straight at us. The next thing I knew our car had flipped over, the children and I were sprawled over the highway, and my husband—he was dead. My happily-ever-after world was shattered.

Certainly the outpouring of love from family and friends helped put the pieces back together. So many people were willing to give of themselves. There were those who came and finished painting the outside of the house, a job my husband had started just before our accident; those two young men who installed a burglar alarm so we would feel more secure; those loving sisters who brought in hot, delicious meals day after day; those who always had a kind word; those who offered so many prayers in our behalf. All the caring, all the loving *did* help me get through each day. But that was all life was for many months—just getting through each day.

Finding myself in the role of a single parent somehow seemed to destroy all my self-confidence. I had always prided myself in my ability to tackle any job that needed to be done. Hadn't I been the one to handle the finances in our home, to pay all the bills, to figure out the income tax forms; hadn't I done much of the yard work; hadn't I helped with the painting and fix-up projects; hadn't I taken care of the children by myself for many weeks when my husband was out of town on business? Yes, I was independent. Or so I thought. But I hadn't realized how much I, in reality, had leaned on my husband for so many things: for a feeling of security, for a feeling of belonging, and, most importantly, for a feeling of self-confidence. Now I was besieged with doubts about myself. How could I possibly successfully raise our four sons alone? . . . I even worried about the last days and getting us through the ordeal alone. It wasn't long until I was convinced that Heavenly Father had made a terrible mistake. He should have taken me and left my husband, for he would have been successful alone.

Because of these feelings of self-doubt, I found myself more and more on my knees, pleading for help from my Heavenly Father. Miraculously, the answer came, and peace filled my soul. I was important; I was capable; I could succeed. Why? Because I suddenly realized the strength inherent in being the literal off-spring of God. I realized that my Heavenly Father truly loved me, that he was on my side—these truths burned within me. I wasn't alone. It was all so simple. My Heavenly Father had confidence in me. He knew I could succeed, for I was a daughter of God.

With the strength of this miracle, I was able to reach out and not just get through each day—I was again able to use each day's opportunities for growth and development. I could once again live more than one day at a time; I could confidently make plans for next week, for next month, and even for next year. (Jean Taylor, "Happily Ever After," *Blueprints for Living: Perspectives for Latter-day Saint Women,* vol. 1, ed. Maren M. Mauritsen [Provo: Brigham Young University Press, 1980], pp. 94–95.)

This woman did prepare. She graduated from college and was able to care for the needs of her family and overcome her feelings of self-doubt.

Remember Alice in Wonderland?

Alice comes to the junction that leads in different directions and asks the Cheshire cat for advice.

"Would you please tell me which way I ought to go from here?"

"That depends a great deal on where you want to get from here."

"I don't much care where," said Alice.

"Then it doesn't much matter which way you go," said the cat.

He spoke the truth, this cat. Unless we have the destination in sight, we might as well let the winter winds come and blow the branches bare, freeze the roots, and kill the new growth.

Winter is mostly unseen preparation. In making plans and decisions, in learning to laugh and act and greet the day with love, we are making a map to a destination. When we desire to learn and practice secure thoughts and persist in our labors, we are getting the destination in sight. Winter is a season of hope.

The destination is clear and we do want it. And look—there in the snow—the blood-red footprints that beckon us to follow, heading not so much in the direction of a place to live but rather toward a person to become.

Spring

An Awakening

Many people say spring is their favorite season because there is such a freshness and renewed hope in the birth of new things. It is almost as if suddenly the world is awakened from a long sleep.

One year I watched a mother of seven hold her new baby in her arms. She had the look and wonder and glow of a new mother with her first child. This seasoned mother saw in her infant a renewed miracle, a reminder of other miracles, other seasons.

Every morning the sun shines after a dark and empty night. After every winter, a spring bursts forth its newness and freshness. After every rain the air is clear and clean and sweet.

If God can do this for the earth, what can he do for you?

I believe the sun, the spring, and other symbols are a testimony of the Savior and a "new life." They are a testimony of new birth in each of us, a new awakening in each of us. This awakening *is* a miracle!

It is a miracle that we are personally responsible to seek. We are to find out—really *awaken* to—who we really are. Spring can be our season of joy.

In Arthur Miller's play *Death of a Salesman* Biff stands over the deathbed of his father and says, "He never knew who he was." (Arthur Miller, *Death of a Salesman* [USA: Viking Press, Inc., 1946], p. 138.)

Do you know who you are?

In the Doctrine and Covenants we read, "Remember the worth of souls is great in the sight of God" (D&C 18:10). What does that mean to you?

Do we know who we are?

I don't believe we really do. Oh, we make an educated guess—very educated, because we have the true gospel answers. But we have only parts of the whole picture, a picture we understand only by faith, for, "we see through a glass, darkly" (1 Corinthians 13:12). I don't believe we truly comprehend our greatness, and certainly we don't comprehend the greatness that awaits us. If we did I suppose this church would be one of Saints and not sinners!

Look through history at the people who had key roles in eternity. I don't think they really knew who they were.

Look at Columbus. Long before he was born this was said of him: "And I looked and beheld a man among the Gentiles, who was separated from the seed of my brethren by the many waters; and I beheld the Spirit of God, that it came down and wrought upon the man; and he went forth upon the many waters, even unto the seed of my brethren, who were in the promised land." (1 Nephi 13:12.)

Do you think Columbus knew who he was? His son Ferdinand wrote years after his father's death that Columbus had a belief that God intended him to make great discoveries in order to spread Christianity. The stories of his four voyages to America are fascinating. They are about his convincing the king and queen of Spain to fund his expedition, struggling to secure money, putting down mutiny, facing failure to find gold, battling more insurrection, and losing his popularity and becoming disgraced when his titles were taken away.

In his remaining months of life he was in poor health and either in bed or painfully traveling by muleback to the courts of Spain in hopes of convincing the king to restore his governorship and rightful share in America. He died in disgrace and despair on 20 May 1506 at the age of fifty-three.

Do you think he knew who he was? He had a conviction that God intended him to make great discoveries and assist in spreading Christianity, but did he know he had been designated to open the door to the promised land and to the restoration of the gospel? He never really knew who he was, or who he could be.

And the pilgrims—did they know who they were? "And it came to pass that I beheld the Spirit of God, that it wrought upon other Gentiles; and they went forth out of captivity, upon the many waters" (1 Nephi 13:13).

And what about George Washington? Did he know who he was? This was said of him and his compatriots: "And for this purpose have I established the Constitution of this land, by the *hands of wise men whom I raised up unto this very purpose,* and redeemed the land by the shedding of blood" (D&C 101:80; italics added).

And the patriots, did they know who they were? Read what was said of them two thousand years before they were born:

> And it came to pass that I, Nephi, beheld that the Gentiles who had gone forth out of captivity did humble themselves before the Lord; and the power of the Lord was with them.

And I beheld that their mother Gentiles were gathered together upon the waters, and upon the land also, to battle against them.

And I beheld that the power of God was with them, and also that the wrath of God was upon all those that were gathered together against them to battle.

And I, Nephi, beheld that the Gentiles that had gone out of captivity were delivered by the power of God out of the hands of all other nations. (1 Nephi 13:16–19.)

When I lived in New England, the mission president stood on the Concord battleground and said, "*This* is sacred ground. It is the home of the prophets."

Did Francis Scott Key know who he was when he penned words that would become the national anthem for that promised land?

> Oh, thus be it ever,
> when free men shall stand . . .
> Blest with vict'ry and peace,
> may the heav'n rescued land
> Praise the Pow'r that made
> and preserved us a nation!
> Then conquer we must,
> when our cause it is just,
> And this be our motto:
> "In God is our trust!"

Did he have any idea how inspired those words were, how closely they paralleled Nephi's words? Did he know they were meant to inspire and remind the inhabitants of the promised land who we are and who our power is?

What about Ruth of the Old Testament, who pledged her loyalty to Naomi? "And Ruth said, Intreat me not to leave thee, or to return from following after thee; for whither thou goest, I will go; and where thou lodgest, I will lodge; thy people shall be my people, and thy God my God." (Ruth 1:16.)

Because of her loyalty, Ruth ended up in Bethlehem, where she met and married Boaz. She bore Obed, who bore Jesse, who bore David—the great King David. Did Ruth have any idea who she was—the great-grandmother of King David, a progenitor of the Savior?

And Joseph Smith, as a boy of fourteen did he have any idea who he was? And remember what Nephi said? "The Lord hath commanded me to make these plates for a wise purpose in him, which purpose I know not" (1 Nephi 9:5). When he left Jerusalem did Nephi have any idea that his testimony and labors would centuries later help to convert millions to the truth?

And did Eve really know who she was? Eventually she must have, but in the beginning did she? I believe she learned about herself by knowing the good from the evil, line upon line, precept upon precept, as we all must do.

Who are you? What is your mission, your purpose? What is your destiny? Do you know who you are?

My friend Rachael has a wonderful testimony of who she really is. Rachael was born on a ranch in Wyoming to an active Latter-day Saint family. When she was a very young child she became extremely ill and her parents sent for the country doctor. He did all that he could for the small girl, but apparently everyone felt she was dying.

Rachael's father wanted to give his precious daughter a blessing. To prepare himself for this he mounted his horse and rode off onto his ranch among his thousands of sheep. There he prayed as he had never prayed before. He begged the Lord for his daughter's life.

There on his knees, he received the answer. Yes, he could have his daughter's life, if that was his choice. He understood clearly that it was *his* choice, and if he wanted his daughter's life, it would cost him dearly.

There was no hesitation; this loving father told the Lord that Rachael's life was worth any price, even his own life if necessary.

He returned from that prayer, administered the blessing, and commanded his daughter to live. She recovered quickly and was a busy little girl once again.

Within the month, the price for Rachael's life was paid. A huge range fire swept this man's land and destroyed all his thousands of sheep.

As Rachael grew up and learned of this story, she wondered if her life had been spared for a special mission. But when she learned one day the meaning of her name, she no longer wondered: she *knew* she had been spared for a mission. The name *Rachael* means *little lamb*.

Today she is an active, busy, talented wife, mother, and grandmother. She has led a full life, yet there have been no "hall of fame" projects. What, then, was or is Rachael's special mission that she was spared for at so great a price?

For years she wondered if there was something important or significant she had to do. She doesn't wonder anymore; she realizes that her entire life has been her mission. There are important things that Rachael has done; there are lives that she has touched, especially in her own family, that would never have been the same without her. I don't think Rachael is even aware of the most important things she's done.

I think the greatest shock any of us will ever have is when we cross the veil and see that the most important work we did we weren't even aware of. We all came here with specific missions, and we complete those missions day by day, bit by bit. I don't believe we really comprehend who we are and whom we are influencing for all eternity. We are a composite of our progenitors who, while they were here, for the most part did not know who they were. The righteous blood in our veins came from them. Righteous influence is given bit by bit, day by day, and is refined and passed on from generation to generation. I feel strongly the righteous influence of my Grandfather Lehi. Somewhere, some righteousness must have been passed down.

I don't think any of us will really know who we are until we cross the veil and see where we came from, who influenced us, and who we influenced. We are told we can become kings and queens, priests and priestesses.

To the extent of our righteous desires we will spend our whole mortal lives reaching, yearning, stretching for that vision. I love Elder Neal A. Maxwell's concept that we are uncomfortable in "time" because we belong to "eternity." I see clearly that we are uncomfortable with all facets of mortality because our nature is eternal. Somewhere mankind lost the true understanding of our divine origin, and created a God who is without body, parts, and passions. But those who recognize truth when they hear it reach for that divine origin. It is a reaching through many dark winter seasons of unseen preparation. Darkly we grasp for who we really are, squinting spiritual eyes at the vision of the woman that awaits us, the woman in Christ.

But after every winter, the Lord always keeps his promise of spring. As spring awakens new life every year, we also need to continually awaken and refresh ourselves to who we really are. The seeds of unseen preparation have pushed their little heads through the soil. Now is the time to see (with spiritual eyes) what has been planted securely in the soul's soil by a loving Gardener. We need to water and nourish this new growth and awaken in ourselves renewed self-vision.

Awaken the Love for Yourself

We need to love ourselves, but loving ourselves is hard because all our lives we've been cautioned and taught the rules about selfishness and pride. Besides, we also have a clear picture of our weaknesses and inadequacies, and we live with them each day. If we are sick, sinful, weak, afraid, or lacking self-confidence, we feel unlovable.

Because there is no limit to you, you will always be exciting! You will always have something to share. *In all of creation there is none greater than you.*

But the vision of that is up to you. No one can catch the vision of your greatness except you. No one will be able to live up to your limitless abilities except you. No one can feel the love of God for you in your own heart but you. No one but you can have these and other experiences.

Counselors and bishops are overworked because too many people don't understand that no one can solve their problems except themselves. Certainly counselors can give keys to skills, but the problem solving is up to the individual. Loving yourself is up to you. No one can do that for you.

Sometimes we blame our difficulties on causes that no longer exist. Maybe we were neglected or unwanted, even abused, as children. Maybe we came from violent homes or suffered divorce or sin or failure.

When we have only *lived through* these experiences and not *worked through* them, we accumulate feelings of guilt and inferiority. When added burdens come along later we become more and more uncertain of ourselves. We end up spending too much time recollecting sorrow and not enough time collecting joy.

You have to learn to forget the past and concentrate on today. Of course, if a grievous sin stands in your way because you haven't cleared it up with your bishop, you need to take that first step to forgetting the past and go see him. If the past is clouded with other, personal sins that don't require the bishop's help, you still need to repent of them, to make it right with the Lord and with yourself—and possibly with any you have offended. But that's all you can do about the past. Poor environment, wrong decisions—you can't do anything now about these past circumstances. What's past is past; there isn't anything you can do to change it, so don't live on regrets. What you can do is make the best of *today*. You *can* change today and all the tomorrows that await you.

You must learn to forgive yourself. Learn to separate your behavior from your character. Admit your negative behavior without slaughtering your character. Say, "I lied," not, "I'm a liar." Say, "I raised my voice," not, "I'm a bad mother." We always hold court on ourselves. We are always the prosecutor. But if we have a weak defense attorney, we can be in serious trouble. If we weakly hear the defense coming from some vague place in our minds, we may lose the case.

Are you a good mother?

Yes.

Did your children read at age two?

No.

Do they know all the Articles of Faith?

No.

Do they make their beds?

No.

Do they behave like ministering angels?

No.

After a few more questions like this, if we don't have a strong defense attorney we feel tried and convicted.

The strong defense turns the verdict completely around.

Then how do you know you are a good mother?

Because my children *know* that I love them.

How do they know you love them?

Because I tell them, I show them, and I teach them the gospel of Jesus Christ. I teach them by trying to be a good example.

There is a woman psychologist who uses the phrase "give yourself a kiss," to teach the principle of forgiveness for ourselves.

We sometimes get so intense over our failures or mistakes that we tend to forget the good we've done. We fail to pat ourselves on the back or give ourselves a "kiss."

For example, assume that you are on a diet. You struggled daily for forty-two consecutive days and have experienced the joy of each day's success. Then your neighbor drops by a German chocolate cake (your favorite) for your family's dinner. She is just being sweet and friendly, but you struggle to say "thank you." All afternoon you smell it and pace the floor. You even put it in the garage so you won't have to look at it. Dinner comes and everyone is served a piece. You can't stand it. A few crumbs on the plate won't hurt; you've been so good for so long! But before you know it, you've eaten not one, but two, *large* pieces!

So you go to bed hating yourself and saying, "Oh, Susie, you *knew* you couldn't do it. You are so weak, so sinful, so much a failure! There you go again—*another* failure."

Mentally you beat yourself up instead of giving yourself a kiss—instead of counting the successful ground you've covered. You should go to bed saying: "Oh, Susie, I'm so proud of you! Look how well you've done. Forty-two days of successful dieting! All right, you've had a setback, but it's only temporary. Come on, Susie, let's go for forty-three starting in the morning!"

Concentrating on the successful ground we've covered is the only thing that can pull us through our failures.

We also have to concentrate on our good qualities. If you've read my other books then I hope you have already made a list—yes, an *actual list*—of all the things you like about yourself. Not a list of the things you like (such as chocolate, babies, color, and so on) but of specific gifts or qualities you like about yourself. If you haven't done this, do it now, *right now.* If you wait and read on you may forget all about this important tool in learning to love yourself.

There is nothing wrong with acknowledging the things you like about yourself. We are afraid to do that because we might appear vain or not humble. This is a false sense of humility. Real humility makes us so very grateful, deeply grateful for the wonderful things God has given us as gifts. If we don't believe in those gifts, how can we ever expect to be like him?

Remember the Savior's example of looking for the good in ourselves? He told us to become "even as I" (3 Nephi 12:48). This was not a statement of arrogance from one who is perfect in humility. No, it was an example for us to look into his life, see his great attributes, and develop them in our own lives. If we don't start dwelling on our good qualities, we won't ever see them, and then we'll miss the vision of the possibility that we can become even as Christ is. The darkness of winter will never give way to the brightness of spring.

Nourish the Belief in Yourself

Maybe you think loving yourself and believing in yourself are the same thing. They're not. Believing in yourself increases your love for yourself. Believing in yourself gives a vision of the woman you were destined to become. It is the hope, expectation, and trust that the vision will be fulfilled.

The easiest thing in this world for you to be is *you*. The hardest thing to be is what other people (or what you think other people) want you to be.

We all have different assignments in life, and for each assignment comes different tools and materials to work with—tools called gifts and talents.

You wouldn't ask a surgeon to perform an operation with plumber's tools, would you? Would you ask a baker to make a cake with a garden spade? Then why should we try to put ourselves into a simplified, stereotyped image of a "Mormon woman" when she just doesn't exist? Yes, we are all trying to become like Jesus and have his attributes, but we do that through our separate and distinct personalities.

I wonder if it insults Father that we often act as if he and our heavenly mother used the same mold over and over to make each of us, when they are actually very creative.

We can instantly see how ridiculous that idea is. And yet, why do we here on earth insist on a simplified stereotype? The truth is that we are each a complex, unique soul.

Cherish your gifts and dreams and visions. They are what make you unique. Believe in them! Believe in you!

If you don't dream your dreams, no one else will dream them for you.

Awaken to that vision of who you are and what you can become. Think of the Savior. How do you picture him? Envision how you expect him to be. Look. There he is, and look, someone is walking with him. It's you. Think of yourself there, beside him. Picture yourself. Picture your face, your features, your smile, your tears.

Look at your clothes. See the brilliance and natural beauty of the simple white dress. Walk next to him, your friend. This is the moment you've been waiting for, your private audience with him who bought you with his precious blood.

You walk along together, by the seashore, across a meadow; perhaps you envision a tree-lined lane. The sun is streaming through the clouds; sunlight sparkles in your hair. Side by side you walk. Picture your smile, your personality, your good qualities coming through. Picture yourself at your finest moments, worthy and noble at his side. Your qualities have all been heightened just by being in his presence.

Think of your mother in heaven. What do you think she looks like? Ponder her presence. Picture her majesty, her royal bearing, her power. Envision her celestial love, her perfect caring and sharing and concern. Picture her patience and tenderness. Draw this complete mental picture of mother in heaven. Now put your face in that picture. That is the vision of the woman God intends for you to become. It is the vision of the woman who walks side by side with the Savior. It is the vision of all the wonderful things you like about yourself—and more, much more—made glorious and perfect.

Henry David Thoreau is quoted as saying that we should thank God every day of our lives for the privilege of having been born. What if you hadn't been born? Would you have missed any excitement, any knowledge, anything rewarding? Is there someone whose life you touched, even insignificantly, that might never have been the same without you?

To me, it is wonderful that we are permitted to intervene continually in our own behalf. It is wonderful to be allowed to live here and help ourselves. It is significant, too, that no one except ourselves can help us very much. We have to believe in ourselves; if we don't, no one else will either.

My feeling is that each of us has the potential for special accomplishment in some field. The opportunities for women to excel are greater today than ever before. We should all be resourceful and ambitious, expanding our interests. Forget self-pity and look for mountains to climb. Everyone has problems. (Camilla Eyring Kimball, "Keys for a Women's Progression," *Blueprints for Living,* vol. 1, p. 23.)

Following are some things we can do to help us foster more belief in ourselves, to help us maintain that vision of our destiny.

1. *List the good things you have done, and reflect on them.* Too often we see the good things we do as too mundane or ordinary and so we negate their value, their influence on eternity. Remember Rachael and her mission? We must realize that the good things we do are mostly day-to-day chores, but such daily work is part of our mission in life and helps enable us to pass on to a future generation our righteous influence. Don't ever let yourself feel you haven't made much of a contribution. You'll never know how much one word might have changed a life.

We need to list our good deeds and *reflect* on them.

Many years ago when our son was six, he made his first basket. It had been a long pursuit. He can still feel the heaviness of that basketball and remember how high the hoop seemed to be.

When he made the basket, he came running into the house to tell me about it. Sharing his excitement, I said, "Hurry back outside and see if you can make another one!"

"No," he said. "First I have to draw a picture of me making it."

That moment—unforgettable, puzzling—slowed me down. It made me thoughtful. It captured the intensity of human experience and forced me to confront myself.

All of us make our first basket, but do we stop and draw a picture of us making it? In other words, do we think about what we do? Do we pause from doing to reflect? Do we assign importance to the small daily happenings of our lives by giving them our attention? Do we preserve them somehow? (Eileen Gibbons Kump, "The Bread and Milk of Living," *A Woman's Choices: The Relief Society Legacy Lectures*, p. 100.)

Just as we spend time reflecting on a permanent vision of the woman we can be, we must picture the good things we've done. Have you ever—

Written a thank-you note?
Made the first move to mend an argument?
Said "I love you"?
Said "I'm sorry"?
Smiled at a stranger, or a weary soul?
Hugged a child?
Obeyed your parents?
Sustained your parents?
Shared a friend's problem?
Worked in a Church calling?
Repented?
Given words of encouragement?
Made a sacrifice for the Lord?

You can probably answer yes to that whole list and add many more. Too often we think of good things done in terms of worldly accomplishments. Worldly accomplishments rarely bring the peace and belief in self that

Christ-centered accomplishments bring. Ponder your good deeds, and reflect on them.

Reflect! Look for the "ripple effect." Refuse to let Satan persuade you that when your stone is tossed into the pond it simply sinks to the bottom without causing that ripple effect. If you believe that then your spirit will feel bound in chains of hopelessness.

Our realm is so significant that our ripple is and will be felt for all eternity.

I met a woman some years ago. She was single, never married, and a popular teacher at a western college. She watched as her younger sisters grew up, married, and had families. She pondered her own place and purpose in life. She decided early that, yes, she would have a happy, productive, useful life even if she didn't marry. Life had to hold meaning because she believed that the Lord loved her as much as he loved married women, and he needed her, too.

This woman is also a seminary teacher and dearly loved. Students from church and school flock to her home. Day or night you can find young people there, sharing food, thoughts, music, and laughter. Her home is filled with those young hearts she constantly teaches and inspires.

A few years ago she was feeling overwhelmed. She was reaching an age at which it became clear that the hopes and dreams she'd had since her youth would never come to pass in this life. At her age she once expected to have a husband, home, and family. This no longer seemed possible and she was feeling a little sorry for herself.

When she was counseling with her bishop about the possibility of serving another mission, the bishop asked her to reconsider because she was so very much needed there in her community. Before she left his office he asked if he might give her a blessing. In essence she was told through the blessing that hers was a great "calling" to be single. She was told that she would not realize the far-reaching effects of her life on this earth until she crossed the veil, "for prophets have sat in your classes." She was counseled that she could not have been such an effective instrument in the lives of young people if she had had children of her own, but that she would yet be a mother, a "mother of multitudes and multinations."

This good sister has allowed me to share this with you because of her ability to care and to love others. She is one of the choicest women ever to come to earth. The Lord has entrusted her with a great calling and mission. I, too, believe we have no idea, and won't have any idea until we cross the veil, of the influence we have even from day to day.

2. *Strive to improve your excellence.* We already know how important a level of excellence is to our self-esteem and motivation. We need to strive to improve those levels a little every day. We need to be willing to work at most things other people aren't willing to do.

I know the story of a little black girl who made a decision to believe in herself by striving to improve her excellence, a little bit every day.

She was born in the least desirable of circumstances. She was poor and was the seventeenth child of her family. But that's not all—she was also severely handicapped.

Born prematurely, she suffered from many complications. She had double pneumonia and scarlet fever, which left her left leg paralyzed. At four years old she could barely toddle around.

For many years she made the tedious, forty-five-mile trip with her mother to the big city of Nashville to see the doctor.

When she was eight, she had to wear braces. She would ask the doctor at each visit, "When will I get to take these braces off and walk without them?" One-half year later, the doctor removed the braces and replaced them with a special high-topped shoe for her left foot.

As she and her mother made the bus trip month after month, year after year, she would tell her mother of her great desires and dreams in life. Her mother always responded, "Honey, the most important thing in life is for you to believe in yourself and keep trying."

The doctor had suggested a little exercise, to have a family member massage her legs a few minutes each day. But she had a different idea of exercise. Her brother put up a makeshift basketball hoop that he made from a peach basket. Every day she would hobble around with that heavy shoe and play basketball. Slowly she became more limber, until one day her mother came home to find her playing barefoot.

When this young girl was thirteen, she began playing basketball for her school team.

She loved her new freedom and challenged herself to improve. She believed in herself. Painfully and painstakingly she strived to improve her excellence a little bit every day.

Of course no one believed it could be done; the foot and leg had been badly paralyzed. No one believed, except this bright-eyed little girl who knew that to her the most important thing in the world was to believe in herself.

Maybe her mother might have guessed then that this humble little black girl with an apparently useless leg would tackle life with determination to do her best. Maybe even her whole family might have guessed she really meant it when she said she wanted to participate in high school sports.

Maybe good friends and those who knew her well might have guessed she would always do her best. They might also have felt that if her best wasn't good enough, she would be grateful for the experience and walk away having gained something meaningful.

But even those who knew her well must have been surprised when, a few years later, this same girl walked out on the stadium field in Rome, Italy, in the summer of 1960—the living legend, Wilma Rudolph.

Wilma said: "When you believe in yourself, you are involved. You are always in the process of trying to master something. . . . I guess that's what makes the so-called champion: the willingness to strive to improve your excellence everyday."

The Champion

The average runner sprints
Until the breath in him is gone.
But the champion has the iron will
That makes him carry on.
For rest the average runner begs
When limp his muscles grow,
But the champion runs on leaden legs—
His spirit makes them go.
The average man's complacent
When he's done his best to score,
But the champion does his best
And then he does a little more.

Author Unidentified

3. *Match the outside to what you are trying to do on the inside.* Your efforts to *feel* good will be weakened unless you make an effort to *look* good, too. The physical and spiritual effort go hand in hand; they are interrelated and interdependent. Don't be mistaken thinking one will be developed *after* you get the other one in order. So many overweight women fool themselves into believing that when they lose weight they'll feel better about themselves

and then they will "fix up" everything else. While it is true that losing weight boosts self-esteem, *self-esteem is the best diet food there is.* If you begin to feel better about yourself generally, to feel more self-worth, you are more inspired to lose weight. This idea applies to all areas of grooming.

We must try to look good while we are improving. Barbara Smith states:

> It is very unrealistic to assume that the clothes we wear and the appearance we are satisfied with have no effect upon the course of our lives. They do. We all respond to the visual appearance of people and to our own appearance. We must make personal decisions about our exterior finish.
>
> Another aspect of this exterior finish is the matter of manners—our social behavior patterns, our attitudes, and the effect they have upon our relationships with others.
>
> Think about the endless detail found in the variety of patterns that our associations generate. We live in a world of constant change. The most constant thing of all is the continuing change in human relationships. The world of people is like a giant kaleidoscope. A twist, a turn, or even a bump, and the relationships of human beings to each other change and move; another forward or reverse turn and the relationships change again. It's a very exciting, worrisome, satisfying, puzzling, challenging world in which we live.
>
> I would not like to leave you with the feeling that appearances and external relationships are so important as to justify spending all of your time with them. They are not, and you must use restraint and good judgment so that you do not waste precious time or become vain.

What I do want to point out is that your exterior finish does influence your life. It invites people to you and to some extent governs their attitudes toward you. It is also true that what we wear, how we look, and how we think about ourselves influence how we feel. (Barbara B. Smith, "Blueprints for Living," *Blueprints for Living,* vol. 1, p. 41.)

4. *Be responsible for your free agency.* I see clearly how my earthly life has been affected by the choices I have made along the way. And my eternal life will also be affected by many of those same choices.

My choice of friends in high school led me astray for a while. Now, years later, I can truly appreciate the words of an inspired family prayer given by my husband, Steve, one morning: "Help us to remember it is better to be alone today than in the company of those who would lead us astray."

My choice of friends in college inspired me to be eager to be a part of something better. The testimonies of Marie, Mary, Francine, Eileen, Connie, and many others truly inspired me to better things.

My choices to obey or disobey my parents had the same effect. Their expectations for me helped me tremendously, but when I chose to disobey I was greatly hindered in my personal progress.

My choice to go to Brigham Young University also changed my life. I was accepted at several outstanding women's universities in New England (where we were living at the time). All my friends were going to those schools—Vassar, Radcliff, Wellesley, Smith. I wanted so badly to go to one of them and become "sophisticated."

My wise father sat down with me one night as I told him of my grand plans to attend Smith. Calmly he looked at me and said, "Anita, do you want to go to Brigham

Young University or do you want to get a job and go to *work*?" Well, I felt he was unjust and unreasonable, and I sobbed and sobbed. Finally, getting nowhere with me, he promised me that if I would go to Brigham Young University for one year, I could then go to *any school in the world* that I desired to. The deal was made.

Returning from Brigham Young University at the end of my freshman year, I saw my father's wisdom. My high school chums were indeed "sophisticated" now; they were drinking, smoking, fornicating, and some even experimenting with drugs. What a contrast to the wholesome girls I'd become friends with at BYU.

My choice to return to BYU greatly influenced my life socially and spiritually.

My choice to marry helped shape my life as I learned more about myself and expanded my understanding of human relationships.

My choice to divorce changed my life dramatically, and I awakened to the need for flexibility and personal purpose and the purposes of women in general.

My choice to have good self-esteem opened up unbelievable new doors to me.

My choice to marry again brought me a better understanding of how love is a gift of the Spirit and what being "one" in Christ might mean.

My choice to have children has been teaching me about unconditional love, joy, and, yes, sorrow.

My choices to weep, moan, and complain about adversity or problems have brought me only despair and doubt.

My choices to "be of good cheer" have helped me hear what I've needed to learn from trials.

My choices to be consistent in striving to obey the commandments have brought me peace, happiness, and power.

I am an ordinary woman and have had mostly ordinary choices. I try to be open and honest, and I struggle with the same kind of imperfections everyone does. My testimony on this point is simple: We are what we choose. We are responsible for our own use of free agency. We cannot leave this to our parents, our spouse, our children, our friends, or our bishop. Certainly they can influence us, but the choices belong to us.

I am a product of my use of free agency, and so are you.

Seek the Light and Warmth of the Holy Ghost

One afternoon I put my little three-year-old daughter down for a nap, then went to my room to catch up on some reading. Her bedroom faces mine, and between the two is the top of our stairway. In the quiet I heard her door creak open. Looking up, I saw her sneaking to the stairway, ready to descend. I said softly, "Paige, what are you doing?" Slapping her hands tightly over her eyes she shouted back, "I'm in my room, taking a nap!"

Paige is not alone in pretending she is unseen. Elder Neal A. Maxwell writes:

> Nor do we sufficiently acknowledge the instinctive things within us that permit us to achieve, for we do not give credit for the divine placement of those instincts within us. . . .
>
> Having a basic sense of direction about life makes all the difference, because if we don't understand things as they really are, then we may wrongly conclude that man is alone in the universe without the redeeming and living God. Such a mistakenly narrow view can cause people either to despair, which is wrong, or to have an inflated sense of self-sufficiency, which is equally wrong and perhaps more dangerous.

When we understand things as they *really* are, we will understand that each of our lives is actually lived out in an astral amphitheatre where, as Paul said, we are "compassed about with so great a cloud of witnesses." (Hebrews 12:1.) There is never any really private behavior, so there can really be no private morality. And when we mortals are lonely, it is not a loneliness that mortal crowds can cure. We could be in a filled Olympic stadium and still miss Him and home! (Maxwell, *Things as They Really Are*, p. 6.)

It is the specific mission of the Holy Ghost to help us understand things as they really are. Elder Maxwell points out that the adverb *really* is used only twice in all scripture. "For the Spirit speaketh the truth and lieth not. Wherefore, it speaketh of things *as they really are*, and of things *as they really will be*; wherefore, these things are manifested unto us plainly, for the salvation of our souls." (Jacob 4:13; italics added.)

Why does the Spirit speak these things? "For the salvation of our souls."

And how does he do it?

The Holy Ghost testifies of things as they *really are*—the reality of a living God, a true church, and a living prophet. He testifies that the scriptures are true revelation.

And he testifies of more reality.

He shows us the reality of our personal weaknesses. If they are shown to us by the Holy Ghost, we aren't afraid or diminished. The Holy Ghost inspires us to change and improve, even showing us that weaknesses are areas in which we can excel.

He shows us the reality of our relationships with others. If we have the Spirit we can see our part in the relationship instead of looking for the faults of others.

A parent, searching for an answer or inspiration to soften the heart of a rebellious child, was reminded during her prayer of these words by Edwin Markham:

> He drew a circle that shut me out—
> Heretic, rebel, a thing to flout.
> But love and I had the wit to win;
> We drew a circle that took him in.
> (Edwin Markham, "Outwitted," *The
> Shoes of Happiness* [Garden City:
> Doubleday, Page, and Co., 1915], p. 1.)

The Holy Ghost shows us discernment in temporal matters. We can see things as they really are no matter how good the counterfeit looks. Counterfeits are those clever "look alikes" Satan puts in our path to lead us away.

For use as a teaching tool, I purchased three pots of silk chrysanthemums and one pot of real chrysanthemums. I pulled all the stems and leaves out of the real pot and shoved them in and around the silk leaves of one of the silk pots. When it was time for the class I put them on a table and asked which were the real flowers; of course, everyone picked the one I had tampered with and were shocked to discover that all three pots contained fake flowers.

Counterfeits are out there waiting to snare us. Even words can be counterfeits. The reality of abortion is counterfeited with the term *termination of potential life*. The reality of fornication is counterfeited with the expression *sleeping together*.

The Holy Ghost shows us the reality of God's principles and truths. He shows us the reality of answers to questions about the gospel and all other fields of knowledge. Can we doubt his importance in our awakening?

The Holy Ghost is the springtime wind under our wings. He makes the awakening possible. He shows us one of the greatest discoveries we will ever make—that we *can* and *must* change.

Seeing ourselves as we *really* are, is the understanding gained as the Lord shows us our weaknesses: "I give unto men weaknesses that they may be humble; and my grace is sufficient for all men that humble themselves before me" (Ether 12:27).

Seeing things as they really are helps us to see our weaknesses as a tool to work with, as a stepping stone rather than a mountain.

To see ourselves as we *really will be* is to know hope: "If they humble themselves before me, and have faith in me, then will I make weak things become strong unto them" (Ether 12:27).

To see things as they really will be is to catch a vision of the woman you want to be, the woman God intends for you to be. Then you can rise up and never be the same again.

It would be wonderful, we think, if we could get all this over with. Why can't the Holy Ghost show us all our weaknesses right from the start so we can rise up *one* time instead of again, and again, and again? Why do we get only fleeting glimpses of that vision?

Brigham Young said:

> The laws that the Lord has given are not fully perfect, because the people could not receive them in their perfect fulness; but they can receive a little here and a little there, a little today and a little tomorrow, a little more next week, and a little more in advance of that next year, if they make a wise improvement upon every little they receive; if they do not, they are left in the shade, and the light which the Lord reveals will

appear darkness to them and the kingdom of heaven will travel on and leave them groping. Hence, if we wish to act upon the fulness of the knowledge that the Lord designs to reveal, little by little, to the inhabitants of the earth, we must improve upon every little as it is revealed. (In *Journal of Discourses* 2:314.)

It is in the *accumulation* of spiritual experiences that the knowledge of salvation comes. We can't be fooled into believing that through a particular experience, or at a certain moment, salvation comes. That idea must be repellent to our Heavenly Father. It suggests that he doesn't consider us worth much if the "glories of eternity" come so cheaply.

If it is foolishness to suppose that an earthly education could come from the experience of a moment, how much greater the foolishness to suppose that the education necessary for eternity could be had so easily. Even Christ "received not of the fulness at first, but continued from grace to grace, until he received a fulness." (D&C 93:13.) The Saints have been promised "revelations in their time," but only as they prove themselves "faithful and diligent." (D&C 59:4.) The knowledge of heaven is obtained "line upon line, precept upon precept, here a little and there a little." (2 Nephi 28:30.) All are directed to seek understanding of eternal things through study and by faith. All must "grow up" in faith, seeking that time when they can "receive a fulness of the Holy Ghost." (D&C 109:14–15.) *It is intended that our association with the Holy Ghost grow deeper and richer with the passing of years.* (Joseph Fielding McConkie, *The Spirit of Revelation* [Salt Lake City: Deseret Book Company, 1984], p. 43; italics added.)

In order to polish our relationship with the Holy Ghost we must spend time in the scriptures. Studying the scriptures is like finding a survival manual while lost in a wilderness. We can find lifesaving steps that lead us to the fountain of righteousness. We can discover the map to the bread of life. We can chart a course away from dangers and pitfalls. And we can find shelter under the words of the prophets. Elder Neal A. Maxwell calls the scriptures "a seamless structure of truth." I love that.

Did you know that you have been charged to be a prophetess? The testimony of Jesus Christ is the spirit of prophecy. Elder Bruce R. McConkie wrote: "Every member of the Church . . . is expected to have the gift of prophecy. It is by this gift that a testimony of the truth comes." (*Mormon Doctrine* [Salt Lake City: Bookcraft, 1966], p. 603.)

Prophets and prophetesses have always been associated with seer stones and a Urim and Thummim. The prophets see and forsee things as they are and things as they really will be. The scriptures can serve as a type of Urim and Thummim for us.

President Spencer W. Kimball said: "I stress again the deep need each woman has to study the scriptures" (*Ensign,* Nov. 1979, p. 102).

How can we dare be indifferent to reading the scriptures? Or worse, why should we ignore the scriptures and seek survival skills from other sources first?

The awakening to the truths of who we really are and really will be will unfold as the Holy Ghost works a mighty change in us, or in our hearts, that we have no more disposition to do evil, but to do good continually" (Mosiah 5:2). "And by the power of the Holy Ghost [we] may know the truth of all things (Moroni 10:5) and see things "as they really are and . . . as they really will be" (Jacob 4:13).

Weed Out Weakness and Plant Strength Instead

Earl Nightingale said, "Success is the progressive realization of a worthy ideal." I love that! Progressive realization—that is an awakening!

When we're working towards something we want to accomplish, which brings us dignity and respect, we are succeeding. Success has nothing to do with the amount of education we have, our age, social status, money, talent, intelligence, or fame. Success—it's not what we are getting, it's what we are *continuing to do!*

Without our weaknesses success would be impossible. If everybody had total capability and no weaknesses there would be nothing to struggle for, nothing to overcome. Success would not be cherished. There would be nothing to improve on. Reaching goals would be known by some other name.

We speak of that special mission we each have. One of our greatest missions in this life is to turn our weaknesses into our strengths. James Russell Lowell wrote: "No man is born into the world whose work is not born with him. . . . This is my work, my blessing, not my doom. Of all who live I am the one by whom this work can best be done in the right way." (Bartlett, *Familiar Quotations,* p. 599.)

Success in life isn't what you get out of it, it's what you become by it.

Don't you see? In mortal life, perfection as a goal—as distinct from an ideal—is not the most significant thing. What is more important here is that we be carefully *consistent in striving* for perfection. Through our striving we can expect, little by little, that perfection will come. The process is what it's all about. We need our weaknesses in order to implement the process. We came here to this earth to strive, to little by little overcome our weaknesses and master ourselves.

85

Could it be true that indeed we are given a weakness in the exact place where we are expected to excel? I believe this is true. If we examine life it becomes crystal clear that in the strict sense there is no such thing as a "natural-born" teacher, orator, saleswoman, inventor, or anything else. The most successful men and women I know, or know of, have without exception denied this theory of natural-born success. The gifts that are in us were "given," and in that sense, they are natural born. They are not, however, the means to our success (remember "continuing to do") unless we refine them and develop them. They are only gifts, they are not yet skills. It is through our struggles and our overcoming weaknesses that we refine them into skills that lead to success.

First, we have a gift, a talent. Then if we work hard we can turn that gift or talent into skills and abilities. If we then use that talent—now refined and enlarged—to bless others and to do good, it becomes a power.

The parable of the ten talents was counsel for us to turn our talents into powers. Remember the fellow who buried his talent? His lord was angry with him; he commanded that the unprofitable servant be cast out. (See Matthew 25:14–30.) We don't know what that man's weakness was; perhaps it was, at least in part, a lack of self-confidence. His lord was upset with him, no doubt not because he had a weakness (we all have weaknesses), but because the man was using his weakness as an excuse, letting his weakness undermine him.

Let's imagine a different ending. The man had been given money. Perhaps he lacked confidence because he had always spent every nickel he ever had. He may have used poor judgment in the past and made foolish purchases and been ridiculed for it. He *knew* his weakness.

Maybe he had borrowed money and never paid it back. With a life of poor financial management and training and many mistakes due to his weakness as a spend-thrift, he lacked confidence in his ability to do anything but fail.

If he had been sensitive to the Spirit of the Lord, he might have understood that he could be a part of something better. Even if Satan whispered that he couldn't possibly change, he could spiritually have sensed that he could do better.

Then his master came with this gift, or this loan. What could he have done at that point?

He could have repented and exercised self-control. Then he could have read or studied about investing, and sought advice. He may have had a small goal, but with a *safe* investment he would have been sure of a return on his money.

When his master returned to check on his money, this man could have shown him the dividends, and that would have increased his self-confidence. The master would have been pleased and allowed him to keep it all, as he did with the others. Then this man could have studied and planned for more investments, diversified, and eventually earned a living. At this point his weakness could have become a strength, the talent a skill.

From there he could even have taught other people how to invest, plan, and manage money. He had the possibility of becoming financially independent. At this point his strength could have become a power.

Look into the lives of people like Jeremiah, who lacked confidence in his power of speech. The Lord raised him up to be a great prophet. Look at Moses, who said, "I am not eloquent. . . . I am slow of speech, and of a slow tongue." (Exodus 4:10.) And Enoch had the same complaint. How odd it seems that the Lord would call upon men with that weakness, men who depended on speech in their roles as prophets.

And look at Nephi, who grieved because he was to be a leader to others, even to his older brothers, yet he struggled with his personal example. He said, "I am encompassed about, because of the temptations and the sins which do so easily beset me" (2 Nephi 4:18).

And what of Paul, who worked against Jesus with pride and prejudice, and yet the Lord called him to be a great missionary. And look at the admitted weaknesses of Alma the father and Alma the younger. Look at the admitted weaknesses of Moroni and Mormon and Joseph Smith. All these people were aware of their weaknesses. Instead of using them as an excuse, they worked with them in their callings, allowing the Lord to turn them into strengths.

John Milton did the same when he wrote *Paradise Lost* fifteen years after he lost his sight. Beethoven was deaf; Thomas Edison failed school; Helen Keller was deaf, blind, and mute. Florence Nightingale said she had to overcompensate for her wealth. She had to contend with her family and society in order to work in the filthy slum hospitals of London.

Most of us don't have obvious weaknesses. We battle in those dark, private corners of our minds where we sweat and hope and pray no one will ever peer. We dread even a moment of exposure. Most of us haven't grasped yet that our weaknesses are the vehicle to our success.

Hundreds of you have written to me and shared with me how you are turning your weaknesses into your strengths. It has truly been an inspiration to me. These are a few of you who have turned your weakness into a strong asset:

—A woman who had been overweight all her life not only lost weight but is also teaching others how to do it.

—A reformed alcoholic is a tremendous success at counseling other alcoholics.

—A woman who once ridiculed others is now building lives in her calling as a stake Relief Society president.

—A formerly inactive sister not only came back and saved her own soul, but went on a mission to Germany to save other souls.

—A girl who lived promiscuously, looking for pleasures and treasures, is now a lovely mother filling her home with children and real love.

—Someone who served time in jail for stealing now won't take a quarter from a pay phone when it is mistakenly returned.

—A woman lacking self-confidence in public speaking is now the wife of a mission president and speaks all over —in a foreign language.

And the list goes on and on.

Look into your own life. What do you see? What is holding you back from success? What can you do to change it?

Let me share with you a personal testimony of how the Lord will change our hearts and reveal ourselves to ourselves so that we might turn our weaknesses, with his help, into our strengths.

One of my worst weaknesses was gossiping, backbiting, judging, and criticizing others. It was a sin that consumed me. It was a weight, a chain of hell that kept me bound down in my own lack of self-esteem. Those who knew me then would never believe that such a person would one day be speaking out on the goodness of others.

It started in high school with all the catty, petty backbiting that young girls do when they are jealous or feel threatened. In college I was even more harsh and critical. During my years as a young married there were those in my life who encouraged, and even enjoyed, this ugly behavior, and I was very much swept away with them.

But because the Holy Ghost can work "a mighty change in . . . our hearts" I was able to see the terrible wrong of this behavior. As I gained more self-esteem, this behavior was unnecessary.

The work of "unlayering" our weaknesses, "peeling" back the worldliness to eventually expose the godliness in each of us, is a process. The Holy Ghost causes our hearts to recognize and desire to change our weaknesses; then, if we but ask for inspiration, he whispers how we might do it.

One day he whispers, "Don't *say* anything bad about anyone anymore." And so for a few years you work and struggle at the "peeling." Another day comes and he whispers, "It's not enough. Another layer must come off. Don't *listen* to anything bad said of others." So for a few more years you struggle to "peel" yet another layer away. And then he whispers again, "It's not enough. You must not *think* of others with judgments." And so a few more years and the peeling continues. Another afternoon and another whisper, "It is not enough. You must *look* for the good in others." So the struggle continues and again you hear another whisper, "Not enough. You must *express* those good thoughts to others." And the unlayering, the struggle to "peel" away goes on.

If you want to turn your weaknesses into strengths, you must first acknowledge your weaknesses with hope. Remember what the Lord said? If men *humble* themselves, if men come unto him, he will show them their weaknesses. He does this with a spirit of love by the power of the Holy Ghost. We end up feeling *inspired*, not discouraged, motivated to be a better person. Be careful to clue into those feelings. Refuse to let Satan show you your weakness. When he does, you feel hopelessness.

Our prayers should contain the request ("if men come unto me") for help. Perhaps sometimes we should pray less of "Father, reveal thy will to me" and pray more of "Father, reveal me to me!"

We need also to associate ourselves with good companions and to stay in holy places. If there are people or places that you associate with that tempt you into questionable or negative behavior you should cease that association.

If you want to learn to ski, and ski well, you can't stay on the bunny hill for too long. You must try to ski with the better skiers so as to emulate them and push yourself to a more advanced level.

Learn to choose good companions and do not let yourself become contaminated with the counterfeits of the world. Ski with the best. Fly with the eagles; don't scratch with the chickens!

We should also accept our Church callings. Testimony after testimony has been borne of how a Church calling changed a life. We don't know how a Church calling can affect us when we are first asked to do it. But the Lord knows, and he inspires his servants in ward leadership to think of you when he wants you in a certain calling. Of this, too, I bear testimony.

If we accept that calling, then he can give us opportunities to develop our gifts, even gifts unknown to us at the time. And he can give us opportunities to overcome our weaknesses. It was during a specific Church calling assignment that the Holy Ghost opened my heart and spiritual eyes to my weakness of judging others. It was through that and other Church callings that miracles have happened in my own human heart. It is because of a specific Church calling that I became interested in reading the scriptures. It has been through serving in specific Church callings that I have learned to see the goodness in others and to develop gifts I never knew I had.

If we refuse the call to a position, we will miss a great

opportunity to grow. Yes, we might feel inadequate, even afraid, at the call, but if we don't "hide" from the Lord he will bless us and inspire us and sanctify our offering. His work is sanctification. In our human weakness we do 10 percent of what is possible, he does 90 percent, and then he gives us all the credit but expects us to willingly give him all of the credit.

We must also keep a balance as we pursue things of the spirit and personal development. When we strive consistently for excellence we should also strive realistically. The gospel gives us a center of gravity that keeps us from being tipped from side to side. If we become overzealous in any one area, or isolate an area of gospel action as the *most important,* we can cause harm to family duties; too much scripture study could dampen Christian service, and concentrating on a specific commandment above all others could cause blind spots in the spirit. Priorities are important in keeping a balance. No one principle of the gospel should overpower all others.

The spring season of our lives is indeed an awakening to *who* we are and *what* we can become with the help of the Holy Ghost, who shows us things as they really are and as they really will be. Through his help we can discover *how* we can make that vision come true.

One exciting and unexpected bonus of being awakened to ourselves is that in the process something happens in our hearts and we cannot help but be awakened to the goodness in others.

We learn to love others as we learn to love ourselves. As we love others, they in return love us. As others love us, we feel more lovable. As we begin to understand how great we are in the creation of all things, we begin to see the greatness in others.

As we begin to believe in who we are, we see our

missions in this life are not unto ourselves. We see that our influence to others is the same as their influence to us.

And as our souls are enlivened and awakened by the Spirit and power of the Holy Ghost, our confidence increases as we are carefully and calculatingly led line by line, step by step, through the *process* of success. Remember, success is what you are *continuing* to do.

With a gentle spirit of hope we can continue to not only inspire others but also to be inspired and sustained while we are improving.

I have received thousands of letters from readers in many parts of the world. (I have tried to answer all of them, but once in a while the address has become misplaced or lost.) The letters have been filled with your hopes and dreams, failures and fears, sins and successes, goals and ideas, and friendship and love. As you have poured out your hearts to me, you have continued to be an influence and inspiration and have helped me to continue in changing my own life.

Late in the spring of this year I found one night that I could not sleep. My mind and soul were burdened. The weight of my responsibility as wife, mother, daughter, sister, teacher, woman, and friend pressed heavy on my thoughts.

That night, when I thought of you, it seemed that this time I should write *you* a letter. You have been so very loving and generous to me with your friendship and sisterhood. Your letters have been intimate and tender and sharing. The desire to write you a letter in that same spirit caused me to get up from my bed and "talk" to you. The letter that follows is one from the heart of a friend and is in return for all you have written and done for me.

Dear Sister,

Today I find myself in a position of doing things I not only never sought but also never dreamed of. In a life mostly centered around self and my own inadequacies, fears, and wants, my dreams of noble deeds never much exceeded my own personal desires in life. I never even looked much beyond the mirror, much less saw the front door.

I knew *you* were outside that front door. But I was afraid: afraid to let you and others see the weakness of my life; afraid you wouldn't love me. So my life centered in self and self-servingness; I wanted to prove to you I was noble or prove to myself that I could be noble.

It would have been a lot easier to hide away in my anonymity than to risk being exposed. But one day the wind under my wings blew open that front door and I saw you for the first time.

Oh, it wasn't that I hadn't seen you ever. Often from out of my protective windowpane from which I viewed the world, I saw you pass my way. We even spoke occasionally through that window which would expose only what I chose to let you see. It seemed like safety to me then, but now I see clearly it was confinement. Living in such a place we can never realize how our weaknesses are turned into our strengths.

But this time, I saw you as I saw myself—a struggling and heavily burdened soul yearning to see the purpose in her life; not the Sunday School lesson kind of purpose that says "to prove yourself and to get a body," but the purpose in specifically being a woman, a daughter, a sister!

And I saw for the first time your sorrow and joy, your confused glance, your worried brow, your gray hair, your careworn hands and feet, your broken heart; I looked past imperfection into your heart and saw a love for the same God I love. *And for the first time I realized that you and I want the same thing—purpose— not for ourselves, but to please him, because we love him.* And suddenly, as I walked farther out of the front door and onto the porch of life, I saw how much he loves his daughters, not in a generalized "God loves all his children," but in a specific, sweet, and special love for his precious and adorable daughters.

My heart nearly burst at the joy of being out of selfish confinement into the fresh air created by a loving Savior. If that door had never blown open I would not have seen those significant footsteps in the path beyond the porch.

Of all the women that could be writing books, giving talks, inspiring others to find self-esteem through loving God and serving him I was the most unlikely. There were so many more worthy women, women who have lived lives above reproach; impeccable lives. Why is it that such a spirit that learned many things the hard way is now speaking out on service and self-esteem? Is it because I am willing to risk the exposure because I have a testimony that the Lord will turn our weaknesses into our strengths? Or is it because I can relate to your discouragement, your divorce, your guilt, your wayward child, your single life, your one-parent home, your crowded moments, your empty places, your fears and broken hearts— because I've been there? Or is it because the Lord wants to prove that only he can change us and that's what makes him God. His way, his path, his road is perfect. All the people around us, all the anti-depressant drugs, all the philosophies of the world won't change us as a loving Father in Heaven can.

He took an unpolished person and inspired her to

catch a vision of what women can become. If he could do that for me, what will he do for you, such a noble and willing spirit?

I don't even know your name and here I share with you a very open testimony of my knowledge that our love for God is the same, and his love for us is perfect and special. Your cares and burdens have become mine; many of my tears are salted with your tears. Never again will I be alone in my grief or trials, for there you are, standing in the shadow of the front door, ever beckoning, ever reminding me that others needs are greater than my own. If I have no shoes, there is always someone with no feet.

You who remain nameless may think that names and introductions are the only way to begin a bond of loyalty. But how can names and introductions mean much "here", when once "there" I called you *sister*?

Nameless sister, the way to ease your care and burden is not a hidden route. I am travelling that way now. Wouldn't it be nice if somehow we could travel that path together hand in hand? It would be wonderful to hold you in my arms and wipe away your tears. I have only two hands, and they cannot meet all the demands to whom my heart responds. But we can find that path alone. We have only to open the front door of our confinements and look past the porch of life. It is the path directly ahead. It is very straight and it has deeply embedded in it, you know, those significant footprints.

And if you stand in the quiet stillness there—the stillness of a new beginning, a new dawn—you will hear the wind under your wings whisper, "My sheep hear my voice, and I know them, and they follow me."

With love and devotion,

Anita

The spring wind will blow fresh life through your fields of vision. A new beginning will come. Spring will be a season of joy—joy in loving yourself enough to change weakness into strength, and joy in realizing it is possible to follow the Savior home.

Summer

A Refinement

*L*iving in the Southwest I have experienced summers of unbearable heat. The summer days in Las Vegas have often reached over 115 degrees, and they were scorching days. In Houston, Texas, one summer it was 95 degrees temperature and 95 percent humidity. I said it was unbearable heat. Another summer we went to Mexico, and in a small inland town it was 124 degrees—and I said *that* was unbearable heat.

Yet I didn't die; the heat really wasn't unbearable, because I did bear it. Isn't it interesting that in the scriptures we find that *heat* is synonymous with *refinement*—as in *refiner's fire*. Looking up the word *summer* in the dictionary brought me a staggering surprise. I was stunned as I read "summer: a period of maturing powers."

Just as the heat of the summer matures the crop and the orchard and makes possible the harvest, so does the heat of refinement in our lives make possible the harvest, the gathering in, the spiritual maturity of the Savior's flock.

It is the gathering he wants to do, that he looks forward to doing, if we will but let him, if we will but submit to him. "How oft will I gather you as a hen gathereth her chickens under her wings, if ye will repent and return unto me" (3 Nephi 10:6).

Whether it is walking *toward* him, leaving behind our worldly possessions and status, or whether it is returning to him by forsaking our wrong attitudes and weaknesses that we have acquired over the years, our test of submission is always the same.

To submit is to be refined, to become more and more like him. Elder Neal A. Maxwell, to whose April 1985 general conference address I am indebted for much of the structure and thought behind this chapter, writes that spiritual submissiveness is so much more than bended knee or bowed head. It is surrender, complete surrender, to the will and mind of God.

> Spiritual submissiveness means . . . we then spend much less time deciding, and much more time serving [the Lord]. . . .
>
> Yielding one's heart to God signals the last stage in our spiritual development. Only then are we beginning to be fully useful to God! How can we sincerely pray to be an instrument in His hands if the instrument seeks to do the instructing? . . .
>
> Submissiveness also checks our tendency to demand advance explanations of the Lord as a perplexed yet trusting Nephi understood: "I know that [God] loveth his children; nevertheless, I do not know the meaning of all things." (1 Nephi 11:17.)
>
> So did a wondering but submissive Mary: ". . . Behold the handmaid of the Lord; be it unto me according to thy word." (Luke 1:38.) (*Ensign*, May 1985, p. 71.)

Directly opposed to this principle of submission are worldly ideas that invite us to think only of ourselves: "For all you do, this one's for you." "You deserve a break today." "You only go around once, grab all." "Relief is just a swallow away." "Why wait?"

This world seems obsessed with immediate sensual gratification. Many want love without commitment, sex without love, benefit packages without responsibility. Pain, labor, and sacrifice are now unacceptable. If it feels good, do it, try it. We want it now.

This superficial view of life won't do, unless we have made a mistake about this mortal experience and think of it, as Elder Maxwell writes "only as [a] coming here to get a body, as if we were merely picking up a suit at the cleaners. Or, lest we casually recite how we have come here to be proved, as if a few brisk push-ups and deep knee bends would do."

We keep forgetting that a test must really be a test, and a trial, really a trial. We fail to remember that when these things come, they have been carefully shaped by the Master Designer. If we look into the shaped experience God designed for his Only Begotten Son, we see that, yes, he had one child without sin, but never one without suffering.

He is the sculptor of our lives, and sorrow is the sculptor's knife that carves our hearts into a shape that allows us to hold more humility and more love.

But this masterpiece cannot be started until we give him our hearts, totally and willingly. This is what he requires, and what we *all* eventually must do. "Behold, the Lord *requireth* the heart" (D&C 64:34; italics added).

If we are meek, a rich and needed insight can be contained in reproof. A new calling can beckon us away from comfortable routine and competencies already acquired. One may be stripped of accustomed luxury in order that the malignant role of materialism be removed. One may feel humiliated in order that pride be chipped away.

The shaping goes on, and it is anything but merely cosmetic. (Neal A. Maxwell, *Ensign*, May 1985, p. 72.)

In this same address, Elder Maxwell noted three Book of Mormon scriptures in striking parallel that describe a "seamless litany" of qualities that bring out submissiveness. (See Mosiah 3:19; Alma 7:23; and Alma 13:28.)

These qualities are meekness, humility, patience, and love, especially a fullness of love.

For the natural man is an enemy to God, and has been from the fall of Adam, and will be, forever and ever, unless he yields to the enticings of the Holy Spirit, and putteth off the natural man and becometh a saint through the atonement of Christ the Lord, and becometh as a child, *submissive, meek, humble, patient, full of love, willing to submit* to all things which the Lord seeth fit to inflict upon him, even as a child doth submit to his father. (Mosiah 3:19.)

Submission Through Meekness

What is meekness? The Savior was described as being meek. Today we think of a meek person as a weak person. But real meekness is *strength turned tender*. To be meek is to acknowledge the reality of God, his love for us, and our dependency on him. Meekness is the morning rays of the summer sun.

My husband has a rock he found in a river bed that is a wonderful visual aid of how strength can be turned tender. It looks like the accompanying sketch.

It is obvious from looking at this rock and its unusual shape that it was in the water for a long time—a hundred years, maybe even longer. When my husband discovered it, all that was above the water was the small flat part at the top of the shaft. The rock is a strength, and yet it submitted to the water, to the flow of the river around it. It wasn't lying on the bottom, out of the way of the current. It was not tossed along with other rocks downstream. Something obviously held it in its place. And as it was held in place those many years, the river was permitted to flow around it, shaping it and carving it into a unique form. This little rock has character. It is unlike any of the other rocks that were in that riverbed.

We are strong and capable of being refined. We can be held firmly in place by accepting God and his love for us and our dependency, complete dependency, on him. This acceptance and trust in him will hold us securely as we are buffeted and shaped by the flow of life around us, As we submit to the experiences the Master Sculptor wishes us to have—experiences he knows will give us character, the true character we seek, the character of God!

"Meekness requires genuine intellectual honesty,

owning up to the learning experiences of the past and listening to the Holy Ghost as he preaches to us from the pulpit of memory." (Neal A. Maxwell, *Ensign*, May 1985, p. 71.)

This means remembering our past sins and our past experiences and being honest with ourselves in applying them to our lives today. It means remembering them with proper perspective.

If we are really honest with ourselves, we will see ourselves as we really are—sinners, with sins of omission as well as commission—and, we will see that we desperately need the outstretched arms of the Savior to bring us safely home.

I used to think sin meant the obvious—stealing, cheating, and so on. But giving up these sins is the easy part of the refinement process. That's when the Sculptor takes the hunk of rock from the ground and knocks off the big protrusions.

Refinement comes when he starts chiseling on the details—the fingers and toes and eyelashes. "The submissive soul will be led aright, enduring some things well while being anxiously engaged in setting other things right—all the time discerning the difference" notes Elder Maxwell.

If we are really honest we will look into our past experiences to help us identify the areas of submission and refinement for today. But too often we hold back.

Sometimes we hold back from yielding to God because we lack faith. Sometimes we don't surrender because we become too caught up in the things of the world, or too entangled in the cares of the world.

Maybe we are slow to yield because we fear, out of understanding *how* the Lord tutors us, what further yielding might bring.

Or maybe we hold back because looking back from the "pulpit of memory" is too full of regrets.

According to Elder Maxwell, "Owning up to the learning experiences of the past and listening to the Holy Ghost as he preaches to us from the pulpit of memory" is to make the best of our regrets.

Our strength can be turned to weakness instead of meekness if we let our regrets consume us, or if we let the past learning experiences become, as Elder Maxwell says, a few brisk push-ups or deep knee bends.

The best way to handle our regrets and past experiences is to let them arouse in us a spirit of conquest. Then we can feel our strength without being diminished.

We have to know our strength and capability and yet at the same time have a tenderness of spirit, a willingness to submit. Looking back into the past gives us a point of reference and place from which to reevaluate.

There is a story about some grubs that lived in the bottom of a pond. One of those grubs learned the value of making the best of his regrets.

It seems that these grubs at the bottom of the pond couldn't understand why none of their friends returned after they had crawled up to the top of the lilies and disappeared above the water. They promised each other one day that the next one that left would return and tell the others what happened up there.

One day the urge to climb the stem to the top overcame one of the grubs. Up he went and disappeared from the sight of his friends. He sat on the lily pad and suddenly began to feel a change come over him. He was transformed into a dragonfly with beautiful wings! He could hardly wait to return to his friends and show them what happened.

He tried to return. He was filled with regret as he flew back and forth across the pond in desperation. Then, he saw his reflection in the pond and realized that even if he could keep his promise, his friends wouldn't recognize him in his new radiance. So away he flew, knowing that they would understand someday when it was their turn. Away he flew, making the best of his regrets.

My regrets are many, but I've been trying to make the best of them. I've written about them in all my books. You don't see them as regrets, but as testimonies that the gospel of Jesus Christ is the only way to happiness and success. The Savior gets all the credit.

Meekness is strength turned tender. It is the morning rays of the summer sun. Bruce R. McConkie became the man he was out of a strength turned tender. I'm sure he relied on past learning experiences and making the most of his regrets to provide him with a spirit of conquest.

He battled cancer for a year and a half. He knew after his surgery in January 1984 that he did not have long to live. But he was meek and submissive, even viewing his trials as a blessing.

"I am quite overwhelmed by deep feelings of thanksgiving and rejoicing for the goodness of the Lord to me," he said in April 1984 general conference. "He has permitted me to suffer pain, feel anxiety, and taste his healing power." (*Ensign*, May 1984, p. 32.)

During his last year he continued heavily in the pursuit of his duties in his apostolic office. In October 1984 he began to deteriorate rapidly, but in the April 1985 conference he rose from his sick bed and bore a witness of Christ that left no doubt: *he knew*. The words he spoke are forever recorded and are scriptures themselves. (See *Ensign*, May 1985, p. 11.)

During his struggle with cancer he demonstrated faith that he would live until his mission was over. Even near the end he would get up, dress, and lie on the bed fully dressed. A family member said, "To him, getting under the covers would have symbolized that he had given up" ("Elder Bruce R. McConkie: 'Preacher of Righteousness,'" *Ensign*, June 1985, p. 15).

A week after that April conference Elder Boyd K. Packer gave him a blessing. Elder McConkie wept and said, "It is now all in the hands of the Lord." He affirmed his willingness to do the *will of the Lord*. Now he took off his clothes and went to bed. Five days later he died. (*Ensign,* June 1985, p. 16.)

The Lord required Elder McConkie's heart, and Elder McConkie submitted willingly and cheerfully.

Submission Through Humility

Humility is the second quality necessary for us to truly be candidates for refinement. Humility is believing that God desires our true development and feeling happiness and gratitude for his goodness to us. Humility is the warmth of the early morning rays of meekness.

The story is told of a little blind girl traveling for hours on a train with her father. A man sitting nearby saw the weary father and offered to hold his daughter for him for a while. "Let me rest you," he said. The father was grateful and accepted. "Do you know who is holding you?" he asked his daughter. To which she humbly replied, "No—but you do."

The trust and acceptance that God is there, and that he not only cares deeply as a loving parent but also is in full control of his orderly creations, is part of developing humility.

Maybe what humility is, is not as important as what humility does.

To me, humility is synonymous with gratitude. A proud person doesn't feel gratitude. He more often feels independent of God and others. Humility produces deep gratitude in our hearts.

Gethsemane and Golgotha were more terrible than anything we have ever imagined. Even Jesus was not aware of the awful agony until the moment itself. Apparently it was much worse than he had ever imagined for he "began to be sore amazed, and to be very heavy" (Mark 14:33).

Why would any man be so willing to give so much for so little in return? The answer comes to each of us sooner or later. He gave so much because he loves us—because he loves us! (See Neal A. Maxwell, *Ensign*, May 1985, pp. 72–73.)

It is in humility that we contemplate his conviction that we are worth the price he paid. A tremendous gratitude then swells in our breasts for his love for us, and we are inspired to be more obedient, more submissive.

If we could really feel deep, deep gratitude for him, for loved ones, gifts, blessings, health, country, home, even for life itself, we would scramble over one another to be first in line to submit.

Submission would come with tears and thanksgiving: "Yes, yes, thy will be done, for look what thou hast done for me!"

If we want to become more humble and make the most of our refinement, we need to develop that kind of deep gratitude.

If you had an appointment with the Savior for five minutes, or thirty minutes, when you saw him what would your first emotion be? There would be only one overwhelming emotion—deep, deep gratitude that he paid so dearly for one unworthy. Gratitude produces humility.

A beautiful friend of mine had an opportunity to look into her own life, into her own frustrations, and discover this great principle of gratitude. She was taught a powerful lesson by the Holy Ghost that gratitude starts by counting our blessings. Counting blessings instead of problems is a *power*, a real power we can each use to dispel gloom. But it's simple, like all the Lord's principles, and people don't want something simple. Somehow, too many have the idea that if a method isn't complex, it has no value. The gospel teaches the opposite.

I asked my friend if she would share her experience of how she discovered humility through gratitude. She wrote the following. (The names have been changed.)

Sunday Incident

One Sunday afternoon my husband and I were spending some time with our family, trying to keep six active children busy in Sabbath activities.

Dave and I were sitting on the couch in the living room listening to Jill play hymns on the piano. One of our teenagers, Kevin, walked through the room and draped himself over the other couch. Another teenage son, Brad, came in to ask our opinion of a social event he wanted to attend. Our two younger boys, Sean and Matt, were playing a game at the kitchen table. The littlest one, Jana, was dressing her dolls beside me on the couch.

The kitchen timer sounded from the oven, signaling that the roast for dinner was done.

Dave and I rose and headed for the kitchen to put dinner on the table. We passed Jill at the piano, inviting her to come help with dinner and thanking her for her playing. Jana followed us with her dolls.

We passed Kevin draped over the couch, joked with him, and arrived at the kitchen.

Dave began to carve the roast, Jill to cut up cantaloupe, and I to supervise the younger boys in setting the table.

As we began to work in the small, U-shaped kitchen, we stumbled over each other at every turn.

We had to continually reach across each other to get things out of the cabinets. At every turn we bumped elbows, and had to say "excuse me." I felt my tension rising.

As I directed the younger boys in setting the table and bringing to them items to put on the table, they fooled around a little, and my tension rose some more.

During this bustling around, Kevin undraped himself from the couch and wandered into the kitchen. He watched the bustling around.

"Mom," he said, "You'd better do something about Sean and Matt when you go on your trip with Dad next week. They really gave the babysitter a hard time last time you went."

Little Jana piped up, "Mom, I don't want you to go on a trip. I am sad when you go."

Her big eyes looked yearningly at me, and my tension went up another notch.

Meanwhile I settled differences between Sean and Matt as they set the table. I angrily kicked out of my path a tennis shoe and sock which had been left there.

"Dave, we've *got* to get that list of family rules made—these children are so untrained!"

He answered, "I'm always available for discussion."

My tension rose again. "You *say* you're always available, but you're not!"

I slammed down the basket of rolls on the table and just then I noticed that Kevin had opened his mouth to join in the fray, and Jana was about to cry.

Suddenly I felt overwhelming anger and couldn't bear to deal with one more thing. The wave of anger was so intense that I was shaking, and yet it seemed to have come out of nowhere. I stopped Kevin's words before they were out of his mouth and I grabbed my purse and notebook from the kitchen desk and blurted out, "I just can't stand this any longer! I'm leaving to go make up a set of family rules and I'm not coming back until I get it done!"

I headed for the front door, propelled by a force I felt I couldn't control.

On the way I was vaguely aware of the children's bewildered faces, and my husband's look of concerned surprise.

I didn't look back but went straight for the car. I drove to a secluded place where I like to go and think.

There I bowed my head, still shaking, and pleaded with the Lord to help me understand what was wrong. "Please Heavenly Father, I don't know why I'm so angry. Please help me."

The thought came into my mind, *Write down your thoughts.*

I immediately opened my notebook, took a fresh page, and started to write down every thought I could remember having during the course of that afternoon. Soon the page was filled as I went back over the moments and replayed them in my mind.

Then I stopped and took a good look at what I had written on the page. It horrified me. There was a long list of fearful, defeated, judgmental, worried thoughts.

I'm worried about Kevin's being lazy.
I'm worried about Brad; I'm not close enough to him.
Our house is too small.
I'll never be able to train children adequately in this tiny kitchen.
Family improvement is too slow; we'll never make it.
I won't survive long enough until things (maybe?) change.

I'm worried about going on the trip with Dave.
What clothes will I take?
Will I do a good enough job as hostess to the other
   people?
Sean and Matt will misbehave when I'm gone.
Jana will be sad without me.
This whole trip is a problem.
The family is so untrained.
Everywhere I turn is pressure.

And the list went on, describing my emotional response to everything said or done that afternoon. No *wonder* I felt angry, upset, and discouraged that things would never change.

With the realization of the cause of the anger came a sudden calm. And then the next question formed: "Heavenly Father, I see what happened. But what can I *do* about it? How can I get rid of these feelings?

The thought came to me, *Write some secure thoughts.*

I wondered. What are secure thoughts? Well, I guess any thought that gives me hope in the situation.

So I took a new page and began to write every thought that gave me hope and comfort that I could overcome the situation. One by one the thoughts came—sweet, secure thoughts.

We can always repent (or change).
We can always grow and improve.
Heavenly Father will give us light and knowledge
   about how to solve our problems.
He will sustain us *while* we're changing.
He will give us sufficient strength to meet the
   demands of *today*—one at a time.
I have many blessings—count them:

A husband who loves me,
  who is willing to change,
  who is wise;
Children who are healthy and who love me;
Friends I could call upon if necessary;
Good health;
Many comforts;
Access to truth through Heavenly Father;
Opportunities to grow.

And the list went on—sweet thoughts of faith, as if someone were beckoning me on, saying, "Come on, you can do it."

The sweetest feeling of peace came over me. Suddenly the anger and anxiety had disappeared, and in it's place was love—

Love for myself, my family, and the Lord.

"Yes, I *can* do it."

I bowed my head again, to thank him, and drove home to face the challenge.

This is another story of humility through gratitude. Mary Manachi lost not one, but three children, to Cooley's anemia, a rare genetic disorder in which the bone marrow does not manufacture adult hemoglobin, the blood protein that carries oxygen to the blood. And she asks the question, "Am I to love life less?"

We'd just cut the watermelons at a Sunday school picnic and I was laughing at the kids' antics—"playing" the sweet pink slices like harmonicas, making big green grins with the rind, spitting the seeds.

"You seem so happy," said a woman next to me. "How do you do it after . . . after all that's happened to you?"

Again and again, people ask me that question—
people who know that Louis and I had three children
who died of Cooley's anemia. First Rosemarie, then
Marylou, then George.

How can I be happy? Well . . .

Marylou was born in 1955. She was our second
child, two years younger than our healthy daughter,
Ann. At first I thought Marylou's pale skin merely
meant she took after me. Although Louis and I are
both of Mediterranean descent, he's the one with the
olive complexion. Marylou's pediatrician wasn't so
sure. "She seems to be anemic," he said, and had her
tested. Afterward, the doctor called Louis and me in
for a consultation.

"I'm sorry," he said, "but your baby has
Thalassemic major." In this rare genetic disorder,
commonly known as Cooley's anemia after the doctor
who discovered it, the bone marrow does not manufacture the proper type of adult hemoglobin, the blood
protein that carries oxygen to body tissues.

"It mainly affects people of Mediterranean heritage," the doctor told us. Wanting a second opinion,
we took Marylou to the Children's Blood Foundation
clinic at the New York-Cornell Medical Center. There,
a doctor confirmed the diagnosis. He also said that
Marylou would have to come back to the clinic every
two weeks for a blood transfusion.

From then on, I drove my daughter into New York
City from West Peterson, N.J., regularly. After a few
months, she got used to it. And she had company; 19
other children were being treated there for the same
illness.

Louis and I wanted more children, but now we
wondered.

"Don't worry," our own doctor assured us. "This
very rarely happens twice in a family."

Rosemarie was born in 1959. She looked fine—bright blue eyes and fine brown hair like Marylou's. But something was wrong. One day she'd seem perfectly normal, the next her head would be sweating. The pattern had been the same with Marylou. Finally, when she was six months old, doctors confirmed that Rosemarie would also need transfusions.

So now I was driving two little girls into the city. It was easy to see how much they depended on the transfusions. As the time for a treatment neared, they would tire easily and become irritable. But after their hospital visit—grueling as it was—they seemed happy again. Meanwhile, Louis and I tried to hide our anguish by giving our three daughters a normal life, with music lessons, games, and family outings.

In 1961 our son, George, was born. We had yearned for a boy, and had been assured our chances of having another child with the same affliction were virtually nil. But from the first moment I held my little boy, I knew. Soon I was taking George into New York along with two-year-old Rosemarie and six-year-old Marylou.

Even so, Louis and I were grateful for our four lovely children. As the years passed, the transfusions became part of our lives, and we went on hoping that a medical breakthrough would make them unnecessary.

Then came our shocking discovery. One morning at the hospital one of the other mothers handed me a newspaper clipping headlined BAFFLING, FATAL BLOOD DISORDER. It was about children coming to that very clinic. *"Many die before they are 20,"* the article said.

I couldn't believe it. I asked our doctor, "Is it true?"

"Yes," he sighed. "I'm afraid it is." There was no

known medical help to prevent my children's death at a young age.

For years Louis and I lived in a daze. His reaction was to say little and concentrate on his work as a garment designer. Mine was to cry whenever I was alone or with the other mothers at the clinic.

We couldn't bring ourselves to discuss it with the children, though I knew that from talking with the other patients, they understood the seriousness of their condition. Then came one of those small but significant moments that change the way you see things.

I'd walked into nine-year-old Rosemarie's room one evening and found her making a jeweled butterfly pin. "How beautiful," I said as I watched her carefully set a rhinestone. She was already selling her work at craft shows.

"Thanks, Mom," she murmured. "I'm going to earn all I can toward college."

College?

I cleared my throat. "Uh . . . what are you planning to study, Honey?"

She looked up, eyes shining. "Nursing, Mom. I want to be like those nice women at the hospital."

She turned back to her work, and I walked slowly out of the room, trying to take it all in. Rosemarie was *not* thinking about death; she was focusing on life.

At Thanksgiving, one of her teachers phoned me. The students had been asked to write about what they were most thankful for. "I thought you'd like to hear Rosemarie's answer," the teacher said. Her voice trembled as she read, "I thank God for my good health."

Good health? How could she write that? Then I remembered the other children Rosemarie saw in the hospital, the ones with amputations or cancer. Rosemarie could walk, go to school, skip rope.

Rosemarie had filled our house with Scripture plaques that she made. In her own room she'd hung one that read: *This is the day which the Lord has made; let us rejoice and be glad in it* (Psalm 118:24).

I saw then that our house was not a house of shadows and sorrow; our children filled it with cheer. Marylou's piano music rang through the rooms. Rosemarie busily crafted jewelry and plaques. Little George had an extensive rock collection; he was already talking about becoming a geologist. Slowly, I began to see that my children, all of them, were rejoicing in life.

On July 4, 1969, Rosemarie, now ten, was in the hospital with a cardiac problem, a side effect of Cooley's. "You seem better, Honey," I said to her that night as I kissed her good-by. "I'll be back in the morning with Daddy."

Just after I got home, the telephone rang. Rosemarie was gone. "Peacefully," the hospital said.

We mourned. My faith was profoundly shaken. . . . Then little by little, I came to a true understanding and discovered life *can* go on.

Marylou and George had known their lives would be short, but with Rosemarie gone they were forced to face the fact head-on. Marylou, four years older than Rosemarie, began carefully tending her sister's grave. I knew she must be contemplating her own death. And yet she took up life with new vitality. She began making the honor roll in high school and was very popular. . . .

In 1973 Marylou graduated from high school as a member of the National Honor Society. . . . In the fall she entered William Paterson College as a fine-arts major. Soon she made the dean's list. She worked part time in a TV repair shop, and her civic activities—collecting for charity, and other volunteer work—put her in touch with almost everyone in town. . . .

Marylou was 19 that Christmas of 1974. In January, our Christmas tree was still up. For some reason I just couldn't take it down.

On January 20, a heavy snow kept us all at home. Marylou practiced her piano in the morning, but she was exhausted. "I think I'll rest for a while," she said as she went to bed. Later I brought her some lunch.

"Oh, this soup is so *good!*" she exclaimed. Then the light went out of her eyes, and she fell back on her pillow.

Marylou's funeral was one of the largest ever in West Paterson. The mayor and the entire city council were there. In the words of the Cooley's volunteer group who honored her, she had "lived and understood life better in her 19 years than most of us could possibly hope to if we lived to be a hundred."

Later, as a cold February rain battered our living room window, I sat thinking about this radiant daughter. On the wall were three plaques Rosemarie had made. *I will never leave thee, nor forsake thee* (Hebrews 13:5). *Casting all your care upon him; for he careth for you* (1 Peter 5:7). *Do not be anxious about tomorrow* (Matthew 6:34). The words wavered in my vision, then cleared. I got up immediately and began preparing dinner for my family.

Our oldest daughter, Ann, was busy with her career. George, a typical teen-ager, kept our house lively. His friends came and went, and the telephone rang constantly. He dated and had an after-school job at a restaurant. After graduating from high school, George went on to William Paterson College. He continued working, and the summer he was 19 he bought a Chevrolet Monza sports car, shiny black with fire-engine-red trim—a young man's dream. He kept it carefully garaged and in showroom shape.

That's why, one night in September 1980, I knew something was wrong. George came home from a date, and after he went to bed I noticed that his Monza was pulled into the garage at a careless angle. A few days later he told me, "Mom, I just can't make it anymore. I'm so tired."

That night he said, "I know I'm going, Mom." He looked at me. "Promise me you won't cry? You know where I'll be."

"No, Georgie, I won't cry."

My son smiled, shook his head and lay back, eyes closed. Then he took a deep breath and was gone.

Rosemarie.
Marylou.
George.

And so, again and again, people ask, "How can you be happy after all that's happened?"

I'll tell you how.

My children understood that life is a holy gift. They loved each day they were given, and their enjoyment and gratitude were like sunlight, warming and brightening our time together. In the face of early death, they embraced life. If they loved life so much—honoring it, reaching out to soothe their stricken friends, using their days creatively—am *I* to love life less?

No! I will not dishonor God—or my children—with gloom and self-pity. I will embrace life as they did. I shall embrace life as they did. I shall rejoice and be glad in it. (Mary Manachi, "Am I to Love Life Less?" *Reader's Digest,* May 1985, pp. 9–16. "Am I to Love Life Less?" was originally published in *Guideposts* magazine as "Loving Life Enough." Copyright © 1985 by Guideposts Associates, Inc., Carmel, New York 10512.)

Submission Through Patience

Another quality mentioned in Mosiah 3:19 that is critical to our submission and refinement is patience. Jesus had to carry the cross before he could wear the crown.

No one ever does his best in life until he has suffered, "for if they never should have bitter they could not know the sweet" (D&C 29:39). Patience is the full intensity from the summer sun and heat.

I've always felt a little cheated, a little let down when the teller of a story or a funny experience or a spiritual moment, frustrated at conveying the spirit of the event, says, "You had to be there." Somehow you *know* you have missed something; you just don't quite know what it is.

Imagine us in the premortal life when, after the announcement of the great plan, we shouted for joy. But suppose a few of us were too impatient to return home, so we decided not to go at all. Imagine further that those who went to mortality could then return to us and describe what it was like. Can you imagine the frustration at trying to explain the principle of the bitter and the sweet to someone who had never experienced either? In complete frustration they would give up and say, "Well, you *had* to be there!" We would know we missed something; we just wouldn't be sure what it was.

Imagine how sad those words would be if, after this life was over and we had refused to bear our afflictions and this life patiently, we met the Gatekeeper and he reminded us sorrowfully, "I'm sorry, you *had* to be there."

Haven't you wished you had been there when you've heard about some wonderful experience you missed?

We can be here, fully present, now.

We can have a wonderful experience, but patience is the key.

Do you remember the story of Peter Pan? When Captain Hook wanted him to walk the plank, Peter Pan said, "Death will be an awfully big adventure!"

Elder Neal A. Maxwell calls this mortal life "high adventure!" And that it is!

I wonder how many great experiences, how many high adventures, I have missed in the past because I lay in bed with the sheets over my head. What did I miss because of impatience with the Lord and myself, because I was not willing to submit?

We ought to insist to ourselves that we will have some great experiences as we go on in life, some high adventure.

We hear the phrase *hang in there*. What in the world does that mean? How I hate to hear that said to me; I am not going to hang in anywhere! This is what we came for: the hard work, the tests, the trials, the submission. When we are progressing, we're in the thick of these things. We came for the progress, not the before, or the after, but the *during*, the progress.

My husband's patriarchal blessing tells him his life will be a "grand, profitable, spiritual experience." It doesn't say he won't suffer; suffer he has. It just says the possibility of the great experience of life is there; it's up to him to make it so.

If we can grasp that idea and change our view of life to envision a grand, profitable, spiritual experience, then whatever we suffer is hardly worth mentioning.

Let's make some high adventure of this life by learning to be patient with ourselves and with the Lord. In counseling the Prophet Joseph Smith to be patient, the Lord said, "Peace be unto thy soul; thine adversity and thine afflictions shall be but a small moment" (D&C 121:7).

Later he said:

> And if thou shouldst be cast into the pit, or into the hands of murderers, and the sentence of death passed upon thee; if thou be cast into the deep; if the billowing surge conspire against thee; if fierce winds become thine enemy; if the heavens gather blackness, and all the elements combine to hedge up the way; and above all, if the very jaws of hell shall gape open the mouth wide after thee, know thou, my son, that all these things shall give thee experience, and shall be for thy good. (D&C 122:7.)

The Lord was speaking here of a specific kind of *experience*, a higher kind of experience. There is the lesser kind, which we simply "live through." And there is the higher level of experience, the kind we "work through." It is the difference between enduring and enduring well. "If thou *endure it well*, God shall exalt thee" (D&C 121:5).

The refinement, real refinement, begins at the line which divides concept from experience, the *right kind* of experience.

For example, you can study a foreign language and even get *A*'s in the class. You can learn to speak and understand it well enough to teach it. But not until you live in the country and mingle among the people can you fully understand the language, the idioms and local expressions, and the specific voice inflections.

As an interior design student I studied theory, principle, and concept. But not until I was actually working with those concepts did I even begin to understand how to apply them to make dramatic results.

We learned a rule of design called the law of chromatic distribution. It says that the larger the area, the lighter the color; the smaller the area, the more intense the color. In school I learned that the largest areas of a room should be the lightest and small objects (such as pillows on a sofa) should have more intense color.

In theory that makes good sense. But after experience, I learned how breaking, actually reversing, that rule produced far more exciting results. One of the awards I won was for a room that was the reverse of that theory. It has only been through my actual experiences of working with people, materials, supplies, craftsmen, space, scale, architects, and money that I have come to understand real interior design.

We can understand the gospel, and still not *know* it. We can understand repentance, but not until we feel forgiven do we learn of its significance. We can learn about humility, even comprehend the idea of it, but not until we experience the mighty change in our hearts do we know true humility. We can understand the Holy Ghost; we can even believe in him. But not until he *whispers* to us and we listen can we know him and have a testimony of him.

Higher learning is always the knowledge that comes from the right kind of experience, from enduring well.

Enduring well is not a passive "hanging on" until our suffering is over. Enduring well, enduring patiently, submitting patiently has nothing to do with strain, tension, misery, or repression. It has everything to do with meekness, gratitude, desire, and love.

The Savior's greatest example to us of a "grand, profitable, spiritual experience" was in his final hours on earth.

He understood clearly the concept of his mission. He knew what he must do, but as he began to "work through" his last hours he grew troubled. Later in Gethsemane the suffering began, and Jesus "began to be sore amazed, and to be very heavy; And saith unto them, My soul is exceeding sorrowful" (Mark 14:33–34).

Can you imagine? The God of this world "sore amazed"? He had known conceptually what he must do, but even he could not have known the experience of it. "He had never personally known the exquisite and exacting process of an atonement before. Thus, when the agony came in its fulness, it was so much, much worse than even He with his unique intellect had ever imagined! No wonder an angel appeared to strengthen him!" (Neal A. Maxwell, *Ensign*, May 1985, p. 72–73.)

Here was our Savior, suffering for sins he had never committed. He was a sinless perfect soul and had never before experienced the suffering for sin. All of *our* afflictions and sicknesses were also somehow a part of the awful agony of this moment.

In his growing anguish, Jesus begged his Father to take away the bitter cup, saying, "Father, all things are possible unto thee; take away this cup from me" (Mark 14:36).

> Had not Jesus as Jehovah, said to Abraham, "Is any thing too hard for the Lord?" (Genesis 18:14.) Had not His angel told a perplexed Mary "For with God nothing shall be impossible"?
>
> . . . Jesus' request was not theater!
>
> In this extremity, did He, perchance, hope for a rescuing ram in the thicket? . . . His suffering—as it were, *enormity* multiplied by *infinity*—evoked His later soul-cry on the cross, and it was a cry of forsakenness. (Neal A. Maxwell, *Ensign*, May 1985, p. 73.)

Even so, Jesus maintained his "sublime submissiveness" as he had in Gethsemane, a submissiveness born of *patience*. He said, "Nevertheless not as I will, but as thou wilt" (Matthew 26:39).

As Jesus "worked through" his experience, he showed us the great example of enduring well. When he realized what he must do, he said, "Now is my soul troubled; and what shall I say? Father, save me from this hour."

Then, almost as if he were reassuring himself, he said, "But for this cause came I unto this hour." (John 12:27.) This was submissiveness of the highest order.

Enduring well is not at all passive. It's all action. We must go to the Lord and ask him for refinement. Sometimes, as I mentioned earlier, we are slow to do this, slow to yield, because we sense what further yielding might bring. If we pray for patience the Lord doesn't suddenly infuse us with patience. No, he puts in our paths those experiences, which if we endure them well and submit, will teach us patience. We will discover that we won't "die" when the temperature becomes unbearable.

This submission, this yielding, hurts—but for this cause came we into the world. I testify that he will sustain us if we are patient and submit cheerfully.

> And it came to pass that the voice of the Lord came to them in their afflictions, saying: Lift up your heads and be of good comfort, for I know of the covenant which ye have made unto me; and I will covenant with my people and deliver them out of bondage.
>
> And I will also ease the burdens which are put upon your shoulders, that even you cannot feel them upon your backs, even while you are in bondage; and this will I do that ye may stand as witnesses for me hereafter, and that ye may know of a surety that I, the Lord God, do visit my people in their afflictions.

And now it came to pass that the burdens which were laid upon Alma and his brethren were made light; yea, the Lord did strengthen them that they could bear up their burdens with ease, and they did *submit cheerfully* and with *patience* to all the will of the Lord.

And it came to pass that so great was their faith and their *patience* that the voice of the Lord came unto them again, saying: Be of good comfort, for on the morrow I will deliver you out of bondage. (Mosiah 24:13–16; italics added.)

Someday we will look back on this life and see our adolescence. We will look back into mortality with a smile. We will look back at the places where, yes, we cried real tears.

Real Tears

When I played Joan of Arc
I cried real tears,

"Help me, Joan,"
Said the Bishop of Beauvais,
"I do not wish to burn you!"

That's when the tears would come,
Real tears on cue,
Every night for four nights.

When we struck the set
I saw them,
Little dry drops on the black canvas.
Strange, I couldn't feel a thing now,
But there they were.

I believe it will be
A little like that
When the current show closes.
When the set is struck

And the costumes cleared away,
I may drop by with a friend and say,

"Look—when I was playing Carol Lynn,
Back in space and in years,
There is the spot,
The very spot,
Where I cried real tears."

(Carol Lynn Pearson, *A Widening View* [Salt Lake City: Bookcraft, 1983], p. 46.)

Submission Through Love

Last but not least in the qualities "seamlessly structured" for refinement is *love,* being full of love. If we were full of love there would not be much room inside for strife, anger, and hate. Love becomes the summer's shade.

Why is love *everything?*

The Pharisees asked the Savior:

Master, which is the great commandment in the law? Jesus said unto him, Thou shalt love the Lord thy God with all thy heart, and with all thy soul, and with all thy mind.

This is the first and great commandment.

And the second is like unto it, Thou shalt love thy neighbor as thyself.

On these two commandments hang all the law and the prophets. (Matthew 22:36–40.)

The greatest of all laws is to love God. If we love God, we'll obey him and trust him. If we obey the commandments, we will feel good about ourselves and love ourselves. If we love ourselves, we can love others. If we love others, they are more likely to love us in return. When we feel loved, we love ourselves more. When we love ourselves more, we want to be even more obedient. We love God more and can feel more of his love for us. It is one eternal round.

They say the opposite of love is hate. But when it comes to loving God and loving people I think the opposite of love is apathy. Some people just don't care about God or each other.

I saw a news program about a dwarf who had grown up in a world of cruelty. This man had been the brunt of jokes and cruelty all his life. He didn't hate others or God. He just developed apathy. He *really* didn't care. And he really didn't care about himself either.

Many years ago he observed the black people. He saw them using hair straighteners and skin lighteners, and he related to them. *They don't like themselves either,* he thought.

Then over the years he began to see a change in them. He saw that "black pride" had been born. He observed that their nature didn't change, just their attitude. It was a turning point for him. He decided to care again, to be proud to be a dwarf. He discovered that self-esteem was his choice. Today he is helping other dwarfs to have pride in themselves and to choose self-esteem, too. He said, in effect, "I found that if I was to have pride in myself, who I was, I had to love God for creating me, not curse him. When I loved him, I could love myself. When I loved myself, I could love my people. And of course, the next step was to love *all* people."

This sweet man discovered the three great laws the Lord outlined to the Pharisees—love of God, love of self, and love of others.

Loving God is the greatest of all commandments. It increases our ability to develop real, Godlike love, more love for him, for ourselves, for others. Perhaps the three most profound words in scripture are "God is love" (1

John 4:16). If we are full of love, we are full of God, and we are more like him.

A godly, well-developed ability to love has almost all power.

> The story is told of a boy who was badly wounded and was brought into the hospital during a war. Word was sent to his mother that he was dying. She came to the hospital and begged to see him, but the doctor said that he was just hovering between life and death, and that the slightest excitement might kill him. Besides, he was unconscious and would not know her. However, she wanted to be near him, so the doctor relented and gave permission for her to sit very quietly by the side of his bed. With her heart bursting she gently laid her hand upon his brow. Without opening his eyes the boy whispered, "Mother, you have come," and the touch of his mother's hand started him toward getting well.
>
> If we truly love God, we may feel his hand upon our fevered souls, and we can say from our inmost depths, "My Savior, you have come." (Sterling W. Sill, *That Ye Might Have Life* [Salt Lake City: Deseret Book Company, 1974], pp. 29–30.)

The Savior's love for us is as sweet as the shade on a hot summer's day. In the scorching midday sun at my son's soccer game, all spectators were cramped together under the only shade near the field—provided by two small trees. Everyone seeks the shade when the summer sun scorches and beats relentlessly upon his back.

For each of us the Savior is our shade. He, a sinless soul, reached out to shade a woman who carried a heavy burden and said, "He that is without sin among you, let him first cast a stone at her" (John 8:7).

He shaded the sick, diseased of body and spirit; he

shaded even those who refused him. He shaded his friends when he raised Lazarus from the dead. He shaded the Nephite children by gathering them to him.

He was shade to the woman who was sick over the death of her son. He was shade to Peter, to the thief on the cross, to his mother when he gave her to John's care; and to Joseph Smith in Liberty Jail. He is the shade to each of us who repents and relies on his name.

Oh sweet, sweet shade of the Savior!

But he who is the Author of summer knows that too much protective shade at the wrong time can kill the grass beneath. My father had a tree on his property that was full and beautiful, but the grass would never grow underneath it. There was too much shade. The grass was overprotected and not allowed to develop strength through standing up to the heat of an unrelenting midday sun.

We can be much like that grass. A little sun and warmth, a little heat and scorch is necessary for our spiritual growth and refinement. We can't say, "A little? Well, you don't know *my* problems and adversity in this life!"

We are not talking about this life only. Compared to eternity, to the whole of our existence, this *is* only a little sun, a little of summer.

We live in perilous times; these are Satan's times. The seasons are changing. Seasons under Satan's influence are now meant to destroy love of God, love of self, and love of others. They are seasons of very little planting, mostly of grafting—evil to evil, sin to sin, corruption to corruption.

What a responsibility we carry! We are not women of the world. We are sisters. We are daughters of God. Having a sure testimony of Jesus, we are prophetesses (Revelation 19:10), members of Jesus Christ's church.

Planted firmly in each of us are the seeds of other seasons, seasons not of this world, seasons of preparation, awakening, refinement, and harvesting—harvesting of souls as well as of greatness in ourselves. We are indeed women for all seasons.

In these perilous times we must not cast aside the things that matter most for the things that matter least. This is our time. It is the time for the women of the Church to behave with a sense of belonging instead of a sense of separateness.

It is possible for us to function on a higher level of sisterhood. The Lord needs the priesthood on the earth to help him get his work done. Sisterhood is in partnership with the priesthood. As well as priesthood, the Lord needs sisterhood to get his work done. He needs us to operate on a higher level in order to be most effective.

A powerful statement about the women disciples of Christ is found in a book called *Portrait of Jesus:*

> The prominence of women among Jesus' first devoted and loyal contemporaries is notable. They were drawn to him alike by their needs and by his masterful personality and message. They came for healing, for forgiveness, for power to lead a new life, and for his benediction on their children. The timid woman who touched the hem of his garment, and when found out came in fear and trembling to thank him; the aggressive Canaanite woman, who would not be put off by the fact that she was not of Jewish race and faith; the women who provided for him out of their means; and the mothers whose children he took in his arms and blessed, . . . laying his hands upon them, are typical. There is no explaining how that first precarious movement of thought and life which Jesus started, with so much against it and, humanly

speaking, so little for it, moved out into its world-transforming influence, without taking into account the response of womanhood to Jesus. When they were sunk in sin, he forgave them; when they were humiliated, he stood up for them; when they suffered social wrongs, he defended them; when they had abilities to offer, he used them; and when they became sentimental and effusive in their devotion to him, he stopped them. (Peter Seymour, ed., *Portrait of Jesus: The Life of Christ in Poetry and Prose* [Kansas City: Hallmark Crown Editions, 1972], p. 34.)

Even though the voices of women of mighty spiritual strength have been infrequent, the message is clear: The Lord needs sisterhood.

From the days of Eve to the present day, our sisterhood is an association of women who are bonded together by their covenants to Jesus Christ. They have also been schooled and prepared by the Holy Ghost. President Kimball, quoting Elder John A. Widtsoe, said of sisterhood:

> "The place of woman in the Church is to walk beside the man, not in front of him nor behind him. . . .
>
> Within those great assurances however, our roles and assignments differ. These are the eternal differences—with women being given many tremendous responsibilities of motherhood and sisterhood and men being given the tremendous responsibilities of fatherhood and priesthood." (*Ensign*, Nov. 1979, p. 102.)

Sisterhood is the accumulation of power that comes with the presence of Christ in our lives. It is not a woman-based relationship produced from dresses, babies, hormones, body parts, and recipes. In that sense it has much less to do with woman and so much more to do with Christ.

This higher level of sisterhood enables us to reach out to each other, to give, to be strong. It is a principle of unity and order. It connects all of us through Christ and brings us together in an unconditional love and respect.

> Most of us have experienced special bonding moments with other women. When the Spirit of the Lord permeates those relationships, we begin to understand the sisterhood that President Kimball is talking about. (Grethe Ballif Peterson, ":Priesthood and Sisterhood: An Equal Partnership," *Blueprints for Living: Perspectives for Latter-day Saint Women,* vol. 2, ed. Maren M. Mauritsen [Provo: Brigham Young University Publications, 1980], p. 54.)

It seems to me that there is an urgent need for us to move to this higher level; the Lord can't get specific work done without sisterhood. The bonding of women to each other through their love for Christ is not abstract; it is real! To be able to serve him, to meet our many responsibilities as women (cook, laundrywoman, chauffeur, lover, wife, mother, bearer of burdens, homemaker, wage earner, and many other roles) we need support, love, and definition that we can get only from each other or from God.

Because there is so much to be done, we need our differences, our uniqueness, our personalities. We need variety in order to bless the many lives with many needs. Our commitment to humanity through Jesus Christ is one thing that unites us as one in sisterhood.

> There's a comforting thought at the close of the day,
> When I'm weary and lonely and sad.
> That sort of grips hold of my crusty old heart
> And bids it be merry and glad.

It gets in my soul and it drives out the blues,
And finally thrills through and through.
It is just a sweet memory that chants the refrain:
"I'm glad I touch shoulders with you!"
Did you know you were brave, did you know you were
   strong?
Did you know there was one leaning hard?
Did you know that I waited and listened and prayed,
And was cheered by your simplest word?
Did you know that I longed for the smile on your face,
For the sound of your voice ringing true?
Did you know that I grew stronger and better because
I had merely touched shoulders with you?
I am glad that I live, that I battle and strive
For the place that I know I must fill;
I am thankful for sorrows. I'll meet with a grin
What fortunes may send, good or ill.
I may not have wealth, I may not be great,
But I know I shall always be true.
For I have in my life that courage you gave
When once I rubbed shoulders with you.

Author Unidentified

Somehow love transcends all pain and all suffering, and somehow love transforms us into more Godlike people.

> Pray unto the Father with all the energy of heart, that ye may be filled with this love, which he hath bestowed upon all who are true followers of his Son, Jesus Christ; . . . that when he shall appear *we shall be like him.* (Moroni 7:48; italics added.)

The dictionary was right, the summer season of our lives is a "period of maturing powers."

Summer is refinement; it is suffering. Refinement means submission. We must submit, meekly, humbly, and patiently, and we must be full of love—for God, for ourselves, and for others.

> Each soul must—now or later—surrender to God. At that moment the universe becomes a vast home, rather than a . . . hostile maze. Surprisingly with such surrender comes victory, and never have any received such surrender terms. To yield to him is to receive *all* that he has! (Maxwell, *Things as They Really Are*, p. 120.)

The picture I have of going home has changed somewhat over the years, and it's a dream that's taking all the love I can give. I used to think I would arrive home all radiant and glowing. Now my concept is that I will arrive in very worn and torn "clothing."

> I say unto you that if ye should serve him who has created you from the beginning, and is preserving you from day to day, by lending you breath, that ye may live and move and do according to your own will, and even supporting you from one moment to another—I say, if ye should serve him with all your whole souls yet ye would be unprofitable servants. (Mosiah 2:21.)

Few in mortality will ever reach the point of selflessness that would enable them to serve Him with *all* of their souls. Even if we did, as the scripture points out, we would still be unprofitable servants.

Joseph Smith said our "very heart strings would be wrenched." They are not pulled because of cruelty, but because the Great Orchestrator is playing those strings and composing chords of greatness for them.

Each heaven-bound soul must surrender to God, and paradoxically, with such surrender comes victory. Submission to God is victory. It is a victory that brings nobility as it imparts the character of the Savior.

If we are earnestly *striving* to be like him, when he comes back again he will know us. And that will ever be vital, because he is the *only* one who can change those worn and tattered rags into celestial robes.

The summer scorch beats relentlessly upon our backs. The season of refinement is upon us. If we submit cheerfully and with patience it becomes a season of strength and of power, mature power. It will be truly worth the battle if we can discover the sweet, sweet shade of the Savior.

Autumn

A Harvest

Winter is a wonderful season. You can curl up with a good book by a fire. Winter clothes are warm and soft. Winter sports are exciting and refreshing. There is a coziness about winter.

Spring is a wonderful season, too. You can open windows after the long winter and let the fresh air invigorate your sleepy house. It is a time to refresh, revitalize, and even to do your spring cleaning. Everyone seems inspired by the new growth, new flowers, new life everywhere.

Summer is another wonderful season. You may accomplish the least in summer because it is usually less structured than the other seasons. The children's being home from school, vacations, and lazy days make for more relaxed time. The days are hot, but there is more time for doing fun things.

My favorite season has always been autumn because it seems to have a little of *all* the seasons. The nights provide the coziness of winter, and on many days in autumn you can wear those warm, soft winter clothes.

Getting back into routines after the unstructured days of summer is a little bit like the awakening of spring—a new start after the lull of summer. And I've enjoyed many warm Indian summers in Autumn.

It seems as if autumn holds a thick luxury of all the seasons. Autumn is when I "regroup" every year. We begin our new year in winter and basically we end it in autumn. For me it has always been a time to reevaluate where I've been all year. It's a time for looking at the fruits of the seeds I've sown.

The spiritual autumn of our lives is also the only season with all the spiritual seasons in it. It is the season of the harvest. Our "unseen preparation" provides us the grooming in order that we might be "awakened" to who we are and what we can become. The awakening enables the Lord to refine us so that we might harvest the goodness in ourselves, and in others. The harvest brings us closer to our goal of becoming like Jesus. In the harvest— the spiritual autumn—we see a need for more preparation, more awakening, more refinement. It is the season with all the other seasons in it.

The Gardener of our lives prepares the soil of our development. He tills and furrows and plants seeds of self-worth, self-esteem, faith, hope, and charity. As these precious seeds push forth through the spiritual soil, they are nothing more than tender little shoots, fragile stems reaching upward for light and warmth with roots stretching deeper and deeper for water and strength.

With proper preparation the garden of our spiritual orchard is alive and awakened with new growth. What a wonderful discovery to see that self-esteem is the lovely hedge that wraps and turns each corner as it surrounds the entire garden! And look, over there—the long straight rows of faith and hope. And who cannot help but be excited about the seedlings of meekness, humility, and patience? But the crowning beauty in the garden is there —in the center—standing tall, majestic, and magnificent —the gorgeous tree of charity.

Summer comes. The sun beats down with relentless force and the period of maturing powers has come. If the seedlings have not dug deeply enough or reached high enough they will not be sufficiently strong to weather the heat of this refining fire. They will shrivel and wither away their purpose.

But if the roots have found the Living Water, and the blades and stems have become strengthened by the Light of Life, they will not only survive the summer heat but also they will begin to thrive.

Then comes the harvest we have waited for. It is the gathering—and, more important, the sharing—of the fruits of that labor.

"Whatsoever ye sow, that shall ye also reap" (D&C 6:33). That is the law of the harvest. When the Savior visited the Nephites he taught: "Even so every good tree bringeth forth good fruit; but a corrupt tree bringeth forth evil fruit. A good tree cannot bring forth evil fruit, neither a corrupt tree bring forth good fruit. (3 Nephi 14:17–18.)

What good is the preparation? What good is the awakening? What good is the refinement? What good are these seasons if they do not produce good fruit? And what good is the fruit if it is not harvested? And what good is the harvest if it is not shared?

This is the part too many people miss. It is in the sharing of ourselves—in the using of our gifts, talents, and testimonies to bless the lives of others—that we gain our greatest joy, our greatest reward. It is in the giving of ourselves that we have the most self-esteem. And although I don't completely understand how this works, I understand why it works. For when we love and give of ourselves to others, we are the closest to being like the Savior!

> He that findeth his life shall lose it: and he that loseth his life for my sake shall find it.
>
> And whosoever shall give to drink unto one of these little ones a cup of cold water in [my] name, . . . verily I say unto you, he shall in no wise lose his reward. (Matthew 10:39, 42.)

It is an eternal principle that when we lift and inspire and motivate others, we also lift ourselves. This is the principle on which the Lord operates. His work and his glory is to help us attain salvation and eternal life.

This whole principle of harvesting can be overwhelming if we look at the entire garden all at once. We should instead view it row by row, bush by bush. Becoming like the Savior can certainly be overwhelming if we think it has to be done in a mortal lifetime. It is going to be a labor of much more than that.

We need to be "anxiously engaged" in this good cause and show forth exceeding patience as we learn line upon line, precept upon precept. We need to be continually lengthening our stride and consistently striving for perfection.

When Jesus Christ said "Come, follow me," he was referring more to walking in his steps than walking to a place. To follow in his steps is to save ourselves and to help others save themselves, too.

Following in his steps—can you imagine anything harder to do? Is there a more difficult challenge? It means to be perfectly patient, loving, forgiving, meek, humble, and submissive to all the Lord may inflict, even if it means laying down our lives for his cause.

The Savior's life is so much greater than we can even imagine; yet we know it is possible to become like him. He not only beckons us to come, he not only encourages us to come, but he also expects us to follow. Why else would he have been willing to pay so much for so little in return? He went to the cross because he *believed* in us. He believed many would follow him.

How can we do it? How can we follow him into the harvest—the harvest of the greatness not only in ourselves but also in the salvation and greatness of others?

Be thou an example of the believers, in word, in conversation, in charity, in spirit, in faith, in purity.

Till I come, give attendance to reading, to exhortation, to doctrine.

Neglect not the gift that is in thee. . . .

Meditate upon these things; give thyself wholly to them; that thy profiting may appear to all.

Take heed unto thyself, and unto the doctrine; continue in them; *for in doing this thou shalt both save thyself, and them that hear thee.* (1 Timothy 4:12–16; italics added.)

In finding our glory and reward by losing ourselves in the service of God, four important words of counsel are: "Be thou an example."

In trying to be an example, we immediately bless our own lives and the lives of those around us. Read the words of these verses again, many times. They are full of truth and light.

"Be thou an example," and do it by "attendance to reading, to exhortation, to doctrine" and by using and developing "the gift that is in thee." "Meditate upon these things," not just casually, but "wholly" so that your example "may appear to all." Paul counseled us to "continue" in these things, and if we do we will "both save [ourselves], and them that hear [us]." That which we sow we shall also reap. It is the law of the harvest.

In gathering and sharing baskets of greatness, the six "fruits" that will become our example are the ones the Lord feels will particularly nourish our spirits.

Fruits of Word

Be thou an example in word. What do you believe in? Are you willing to stand up and be counted?

We live in a day of changing values and standards, of immediate sensual gratification, of here-today-and-gone-tomorrow programs and reforms. We see this not only in government but also in the homes, schools, and churches of our nation and the world. We even see it among some of our own Church members who are led away by the philosophies of men.

People everywhere seem to be groping in darkness, discarding the traditions that were the strength of society, and yet they are unable to find a new star to guide them.

Barbara Tuchman, a Pulitzer Prize winning historian, stated:

> When it comes to leaders we have, if anything, a super abundance—hundreds of Pied Pipers—ready and anxious to lead the population. They are scurrying around, collecting consensus, gathering as wide an acceptance as possible. But what they are not doing very notably is standing still and saying, "This is what I believe. This I will do and that I will not do. This is my code of behavior and that is outside it. This is excellent and that is trash." There is an absence of moral leadership in the sense of a general unwillingness to state standards. . . .

Of all the ills that our poor . . . society is heir to, the focal one, it seems to me, from which so much of our uneasiness and confusion derive, is the absence of standards. We are too unsure of ourselves to assert them, to stick by them, if necessary in the case of persons who occupy positions of authority, to impose them. We seem to be afflicted by a widespread and eroding reluctance to take any stand on any values, moral, behavioral or esthetic. ("The Missing Element —Moral Courage," *McCalls,* June 1967, p. 28, quoted in Gordon B. Hinckley, *Be Thou An Example* [Salt Lake City: Deseret Book Company, 1981], pp. 11–12.)

The standards of the Church are God's standards. We need to find them and obey them.

We need to say: "This is what I believe. This I will do and that I will not do. This is my code of behavior; that is outside of it." We need to ask, "How would Jesus do this?"

He would not contend with others; he would simply state his belief and then conduct himself accordingly.

In my travels all over this church, I've met many wonderful women with wonderful names—Susan, Sharon, Mary, Alice, Jane, Marilyn, Becky, Debbie, Tammie, Carolyn, Cheri, Rita, Margret, and on and on.

Our names are very much like the names of our non-member sisters in this world, but we are definitely set apart from them because we have taken upon ourselves another name—the name of Jesus Christ our Lord. We share in it. We take upon us the obligation of being obedient to his will, of following his timetable, of helping mankind, of drawing near to his Spirit.

It is increasingly more clear how critically important the work of women is in the plan of life and salvation.

We love, we comfort, we create, we nurture, we teach,

we "feel after," we are responsible for birth, we set the tone.

The Lord needs us. We have never been more needed. We need to be valiant women who are not ashamed of the gospel of Jesus Christ, women who can stand up and be counted.

Sisters, I am excited. There is a major "wave" gathering among the women of the Church. A special spirit is moving among the Lord's valiant women. And do you know why?

President Kimball said:

> Much of the major growth that is coming to the Church in the last days will come because many of the good women of the world (in whom there is often such an inner sense of spirituality) will be drawn to the Church in large numbers. This will happen to the degree that the women of the Church reflect righteousness and articulateness in their lives and to the degree that they are seen as distinct and different—in happy ways—from the women of the world. . . .
>
> Thus it will be that the female exemplars of the Church will be a significant force in both the numerical and the spiritual growth of the Church in the last days. (Spencer W. Kimball, *My Beloved Sisters* [Salt Lake City: Deseret Book Company, 1979], pp. 44–45; used by permission.)

I really don't know what the council in heaven was like, but I know it was a place and time wherein we had to stand up and be counted.

I'm sure it didn't happen in exactly this way, but I like to conjure up a picture of a vast palatial court with a concourse of people, talking excitedly, some even in heated arguments. The Lord enters and the roll call begins. "Who's on the Lord's side, who? Now is the time to show."

In my mind I can see the votes begin to be cast, and anxiously and breathlessly each awaits his turn. Suddenly you're next. All eyes are on you. There is no hesitation, no doubt, no second thought. This is the moment you've waited for. You determinedly walk across the line and say, "I am on the Lord's side."

We should live our lives *here* in such a way that we reflect our votes *there.*

As a young girl I very much loved reading, especially poetry and philosophy. I noticed that many notable poets and philosophers wrote their epitaphs. At the time I thought, *How morbid!* But now I realize these epitaphs were a measure for them to live by, to live up to.

When Steve and I visited St. Paul's Cathedral in London, we read the epitaph of Sir Christopher Wren, who is buried there. He was the genius architect of that magnificient structure and of many other brilliant buildings in that city. The epitaph stated: "Here is laid to rest the builder of this church and city. If you seek his monument, look around you."

What do you want your epitaph to read? Think about that. It should be something that says what your life's work stood for, what you hoped and dreamed life would be. What do you want to be remembered for? What will your monument be?

Write your epitaph. Make it one that will inspire you to be an example in word and belief. Write an epitaph that you can live by and live up to, one that will inspire you to become more and more like Jesus Christ.

Fruits of Conversation

Be thou an example in conversation. The Lord wants us to communicate with each other in word and deed. He wants us to refrain from light-mindedness, dark thoughts that lead to dark conversation, gossip, speaking evil of the Lord's anointed (we are *all* the Lord's "anointed"), and vulgar or off-color words and subjects. He wants us to be clean in heart and thought.

Gossiping is a horrible problem. Some who think they don't gossip are shocked to learn that statements like these—"Listen, I *really* like her a lot, but she . . ." and "I really shouldn't say this, but . . ." and "I never talk about people, or judge them, but . . ." and "I mean, she has so many good qualities, but . . ."—are really gossip. They are prefaced with what sounds like a Christian attitude, but it is definitely another counterfeit.

It is possible to stop gossiping. From my own experience I can tell you that if you look for the good in others, especially when you don't want to, you will find it. After you find that good, *say it* over and over and over. Say it to them, to others, and to yourself. Soon you'll notice it's easier and easier to see the good, and others will begin to look at you as a person who says nothing bad about anyone else. What a good example you will become.

The Lord also wants us to be an example in our conversation through the bearing of our testimonies. It is the bearing of our testimony that actually strengthens our testimony. It also gives us the added blessing that our sins are forgiven. "Nevertheless, ye are blessed, for the testimony which ye have borne is recorded in heaven for the angels to look upon; and they rejoice over you, and your sins are forgiven you" (D&C 62:3).

The bearing of testimony reflects the spirit of prophecy. I remember when some people once "set me up" to discuss the gospel. It turned out to be a kangaroo court, and when I realized that defending my faith simply would not do any more good at all, I decided to bear my testimony. The Spirit and a feeling of power came over me as I simply said, "I *know* that my church is true, and that God lives and Jesus Christ is his Son, the *living* Savior. This is his church." The feeling changed in the room. Later, a few even apologized. The power of a testimony should never be taken casually.

Years ago when we lived in Florida, we met a young couple through my husband's work. The only social contact we had with them was through their mutual work. The husband in the other couple was the son of a Baptist minister, so naturally the subject of religion came up often. In our conversations we never bore our testimonies with conviction, but with timidity. I was too concerned about offending them.

They moved to southern Florida, and we went to Utah. A few years later I sent their name in on a missionary referral card, never really believing anything would come of it.

About three more years passed, and we were living in Nevada. One night the phone rang and it was the wife of this same couple. They would be passing through Las Vegas and wanted to stay with us. We were delighted to have them, but absolutely overjoyed when we learned the reason for their trip West. They were coming to be sealed in the temple.

During our visit we learned of how that referral card made it down to the swamps of southern Florida where they were living, and of their conversion and baptism. But the reason they let the missionaries into their home has made a difference in my conversations for the rest of my life.

They told us they let the missionaries in because they had never known anyone who had believed his church was true except us. Even with a minister for a father, this young man had never heard anyone express the knowledge of the truthfulness of his church. They wanted to know what made us "feel the way we did." He said, "You were good examples to us."

Since that day I have never been ashamed to bear my testimony or worried about offending someone. If done with the Spirit, our testimonies can open doors to non-members. One of the strangers I bore my testimony to on an airplane is investigating the Church. I've borne my testimony to dozens of strangers on airplanes, but only one that I know of has responded. Even if none ever responded, the strength that I have gained in bearing that witness of this special church has given me courage and made me feel closer to the Lord's work.

Our testimonies are recorded. Somewhere in all of eternity, will they then become scripture? Certainly Joseph Smith's testimony has become scripture, as have the testimonies of many others:

> And while we meditated upon these things, the Lord touched the eyes of our understandings and they were opened, and the glory of the Lord shone round about.
>
> And we beheld the glory of the Son, on the right hand of the Father, and received of his fulness;
>
> And saw the holy angels, and them who are sanctified before his throne, worshiping God, and the Lamb, who worship him forever and ever.
>
> And now, after the many testimonies which have been given of him, this is the testimony, last of all, which we give of him: That he lives!
>
> For we saw him, even on the right hand of God; and we heard the voice bearing record that he is the Only Begotten of the Father—
>
> That by him, and through him, and of him, the worlds are and were created, and the inhabitants thereof are begotten sons and daughters unto God. (D&C 76:19–24.)

Elder Bruce R. McConkie bore such a final glorious testimony. As you read it, you get the distinct feeling that, yes, this *is* scripture.

I feel, and the Spirit seems to accord, that the most important doctrine I can declare, and the most powerful testimony I can bear, is of the atoning sacrifice of the Lord Jesus Christ.

His atonement is the most transcendent event that ever has or ever will occur from Creation's dawn through all the ages of a never-ending eternity.

It is the supreme act of goodness and grace that only a god could perform. Through it, all of the terms and conditions of the Father's eternal plan of salvation become operative.

Through it are brought to pass the immortality and eternal life of man. Through it, all men are saved from death, hell, the devil, and endless torment.

And through it, all who believe and obey the glorious gospel of God, all who are true and faithful and overcome the world, all who suffer for Christ and his word, all who are chastened and scourged in the Cause of him whose we are—all shall become as their Maker and sit with him on his throne and reign with him forever in everlasting glory. . . .

I am one of his witnesses, and in a coming day I shall feel the nail marks in his hands and in his feet and shall wet his feet with my tears.

But I shall not know any better then than I know now that he is God's Almighty Son, that he is our Savior and Redeemer, and that salvation comes in and through his atoning blood and in no other way.

God grant that all of us may walk in the light as God our Father is in the light so that, according to the promises, the blood of Jesus Christ his Son will cleanse us from all sin. (*Ensign*, May 1985, pp. 9, 11.)

It is important for us to place the highest and deepest value on our examples in conversation. Who knows who might be listening, both in this world and in others.

Fruits of Charity

Be thou an example in charity. What is charity? It is not what the world thinks it is. It is not tokens, gifts, services, or gestures. These help us to *develop* charity, but they are not charity.

> Though I speak with the tongues of men and of angels, and have not charity, I am become as sounding brass, or a tinkling cymbal.
>
> And though I have the gift of prophecy, and understand all mysteries, and all knowledge; and though I have all faith, so that I could remove mountains, and have not charity, I am nothing.
>
> And though I bestow all my goods to feed the poor, and though I give my body to be burned, and have not charity, it profiteth me nothing.
>
> Charity suffereth long, and is kind; charity envieth not; charity vaunteth not itself, is not puffed up.
>
> Doth not behave itself unseemly, seeketh not her own, is not easily provoked, thinketh no evil;
>
> Rejoiceth not in iniquity, but rejoiceth in the truth;
>
> Beareth all things, believeth all things, hopeth all things, endureth all things. (1 Corinthians 13:1–7.)

I don't yet completely understand this kind of love, but I'm working on it. The Lord will place in our paths— if we let him, if we submit and ask—the very experiences that will teach us to suffer long, to be kind, to strip away pride, to hope and endure and bear *all* things. The learning of this love is line upon line. Charity is also a gift, the greatest of all gifts, and we must *earn* it. We must fill our harvest baskets with charity.

> And charity suffereth long, and is kind, and envieth not, and is not puffed up, seeketh not her own, is not easily provoked, thinketh no evil, and

rejoiceth not in iniquity but rejoiceth in the truth, beareth all things, believeth all things, hopeth all things, endureth all things.

Wherefore, my beloved brethren, if ye have not charity, ye are nothing, for charity never faileth,

Wherefore, cleave unto charity, which is the greatest of all, for all things must fail—

But charity is the pure love of Christ, and it endureth forever; and whoso is found possessed of it at the last day, it shall be well with him.

Wherefore, my beloved brethren, *pray unto the Father with all the energy of heart, that ye may be filled with this love,* which he hath bestowed upon all who are true followers of his Son, Jesus Christ; that ye may become the sons of God; that when he shall appear we shall be like him, for we shall see him as he is; that we may have this hope; that we may be purified even as he is pure. Amen. (Moroni 7:45–48; italics added.)

Charity is the "greatest of all" the spiritual gifts, and we earn it and develop it in action. We earn it by serving others with kindness, without seeking praise or reward, without envy, without pride, without thinking evil of others. We earn it by rejoicing in others' successes, thinking good thoughts of others, and in subduing our anger. We earn it by being patient in suffering, and hoping, bearing, and enduring all things. We earn it by seeking it in humble and sincere prayer.

We have an idea how much effort it takes to develop and earn charity when we read the admonition, "Pray unto the Father with all the energy of heart, that ye may be filled with this love." That is our admonition—to pray for it, to seek it. But remembering *how* the Lord tutors us, we are often slow to yield "because we sense what further yielding might bring" (Neal A. Maxwell, *Ensign,* May 1985, p. 71).

The Lord puts in our way the educating, custom-made experiences that will teach us how to be more charitable. The unlovable often cross our paths. Or a precious loved one despitefully uses us, or a husband or child breaks our hearts. Maybe we are given some tremendous call of service that takes sacrifice of time, talent, and money, not to mention "all the love you can give." Or there are those who offend us, and we must forgive them.

If we want to be like him at the last day, we have to pay the price. It's a price often paid in pain, sorrow, and sacrifice. Developing real charity, real love for others has to hurt. It's easy to endure well when there is nothing pressing heavy against us. It is easy to hope and bear all things when there are no worries, doubts, or troubles to deal with. It's easy to love good and righteous and lovable people. It is easy to be forgiving when no one hurts you.

Earning charity hurts because somewhere in our paths are placed "the opposites." It is through sorrow that we know joy. It is through bitter that we know sweet. It is through subduing pride that we learn humility.

As we learn to love the unlovable and patiently hope, bear, and endure with our hurting hearts, we are earning charity.

What a great example of charity the Savior gave us when he washed the feet of his disciples. Would you let him wash your feet? It seems absurd to think of that, and yet, he already has washed our feet spiritually.

So after he had washed their feet, and had taken his garments, and was set down again, he said unto them, Know ye what I have done to you?

Ye call me Master and Lord: and ye say well; for so I am.

If I then, your Lord and Master, have washed your feet; ye also ought to wash one another's feet.

> For I have given you an example, that ye should do as I have done to you.
>
> Verily, verily, I say unto you, The servant is not greater than his lord; neither he that is sent greater than he that sent him.
>
> If ye know these things, happy are ye if ye do them. (John 13:12–17.)

Dixie is a friend to the Savior; she has served him personally. I've never met her, but one summer, a week before BYU Education Week, she called me from her home in Texas. She said, "Anita, I know you'll be leaving your family for a whole week to go to Brigham Young University to serve the sisters. I can't go this year. I just don't have the time or the arrangements. But I want to do something for you.

"I can't bring your family dinner, but I can send them something. Will you please give me the names and ages of your children, so that I might send them 'good cheer'?"

During the week that I was gone my husband told me of the little cards and notes and trinkets that came. Balloons, books, treats, and words of "thank you for sharing your mom." Our whole family was deeply touched. I've never met Dixie, but she's a special woman because she has served the Savior by serving and loving others.

> For I was an hungered, and ye gave me meat: I was thirsty, and ye gave me drink: I was a stranger, and ye took me in:
>
> Naked, and ye clothed me: I was sick, and ye visited me: I was in prison, and ye came unto me.
>
> Then shall the righteous answer him, saying, Lord, when saw we thee an hungered, and fed thee? or thirsty, and gave thee drink?
>
> When saw we thee a stranger, and took thee in? or naked, and clothed thee?

Or when saw we thee sick, or in prison, and came unto thee?

And the King shall answer and say unto them, Verily I say unto you, Inasmuch as ye have done it unto one of the least of these my brethren, ye have done it unto me. (Matthew 25:35–40.)

Traveling around the Church I have been inspired and blessed to hear stories of great miracles and charity among the Lord's people. In Kansas I saw a weary brother carry his invalid sister into a meetinghouse to be able to hear the women's conference. He had driven nearly half the night and waited patiently in the car for three more hours before facing another five-hour drive home. To see him carry her frail body so tenderly, so carefully, brought tears of love and respect for one with so great a gift of love.

Charity Beareth All Things

In Dallas, Texas, I saw the English-speaking sisters of a stake go out of their way to make their Lamanite sisters feel loved and wanted. Often non-English-speaking sisters have low self-esteem, feel uncomfortable, and even think themselves a nuisance around their polished, articulate English-speaking sisters. These great women placed a table at the head of the room and seated these Lamanite women there with the Stake Relief Society president and her board. You should have seen the smiles of gratitude.

Charity Is Not Puffed Up

In St. George, Utah, I watched a woman use her own money to tape talks, meetings, and women's conferences in order to establish a lending library from her home. She made this material available to all those who needed and wanted inspiration, never charging a penny for her own time and investment. She personally would take these resources into the homes of the sick and afflicted, those who needed a comforting hand.

Charity Is Kind

In a stake in Florida I met a woman, who, with her husband, goes into the streets and finds wayward youth —the homeless, lost, and rebellious. They bring those who will come into their home and feed, clothe, and counsel them. Certainly they have had a few problems, but from these years of love, sacrifice, and devotion have come many rehabilitated lives, including several baptisms.

Charity Hopeth All Things

In Washington I learned of a sister who was overwhelmed at the needs of the incoming Vietnamese refugees. She put together an organization of volunteers that provided food, clothing, shelter, job training, cultural transition, and friendshipping to these homeless, frightened people. She was filled with such compassion for their suffering that she too experienced what they were feeling.

Charity Beareth All Things

Pages and pages could be written with stories of charity—real love, pure love—of women and men caring for their fellow beings. I've learned of many who take care of their elderly parents, who feel the burden of advancing years upon their own bodies, yet lovingly and unselfishly wash, feed, and clothe their aging mothers or fathers.

Charity Suffereth Long

I've watched and met countless men and women who have left their comfortable homes and security of retirement, friends, and loved ones to go to new places, eat strange food, even learn a new language. All this sacrifice in order to teach a handful of God's children the gospel of Jesus Christ. These senior missionaries are often in poor health and on limited incomes. Their charity is an example not only to those in the world, but to those of us in the Church as well.

Charity Rejoiceth in Truth

"Be thou an example of the believers . . . in charity" —sharing, volunteering, cleaning up, comforting, serving, talking, teaching, listening, and so much more. Watch your empty baskets come back to you with an abundant harvest.

I have seen charity in the eyes and countenances of two sisters: one in a wheelchair, the other taking care of her. I watched them all over the Brigham Young University campus, the one sister pushing, feeding, writing, doing for her sister without legs. It was selfless, and it was charity.

I watched the charity in the heart of a mother with a retarded child on her lap. The looks and stares went unnoticed as she marveled and glowed with pride at her baby's responses.

I know another mother whose charity brings tears to my eyes as I watch her love her interracial family. She too is oblivious to the jeers and sneers as people notice her Mexican, black, and Oriental children. Unable to bear her own, she's opened her heart to the unwanted, unloved, and still most precious.

Charity is in the faces of men and women and children in this church. But it is not an exclusive possession of members of the true church. Indeed, there are many nonmembers that would put many of us members to shame.

Take Annie for example. She is a seventy-eight-year-old black woman who lives alone, and somewhat forgotten, in Oakland, California. For her life was meant to share, to give of yourself. Annie doesn't have anything to give. She is so poor that she doesn't turn on her lights after dark, and goes without heat often. But Annie has a heart of love to give away.

She collects scraps of cloth, old clothing, any fabric she can get her hands on and spends what little extra money she has on supplies. She makes three quilts a month for needy children. The local service groups in her area know they can count on Annie's quilts.

When the local television station found out about her, she refused to be interviewed and told them not to use her last name. In Annie's words, "It wouldn't be a gift then."

Charity seeketh not her own.

And charity has been in the notes and gifts and cards and letters from many of you. Could you possibly ever know how much your love has been like soothing oil poured into the dry, cracked places of my heart?

You are a major source of *hope* in this world for love, the purest love possible, to continue to exist. Be thou an example in charity. Fill your harvest baskets with charity.

Do you doubt your influence?

Fruits of the Spirit

Be thou an example in spirit. We must be an example to others as a reverent and repentant people. We need to develop a spirit of reverence.

Ardeth Kapp tells this story of her father before his death.

> It was not long ago that I witnessed what until then had been something of a routine for me, the blessing on the food. Picture with me, my aged father, his body deteriorated by the devastation of stomach cancer, while his spirit was magnified and refined through suffering. He sat at the kitchen table; he then weighed less than a hundred pounds. Bowing his head, resting it in his frail, trembling hands over a spoonful of baby food—all that he could eat— he pronounced a blessing on the food—as though it were a sacred sacrament—and gave thanks with acceptance and submission, with truth and faith, because he knew to whom he was speaking. (Ardeth Greene Kapp, "Drifting, Dreaming, Directing," *Blueprints for Living*, vol. 1, p. 86.)

President Spencer W. Kimball made these comments on reverence:

> Reverence is not a state of being, but an *attitude*. We must become a person who reveres the Lord's creations and before his throne in humble reverence bow (D&C 76:93). . . .
>
> Many of our leaders have expressed regard for reverence as one of the highest qualities of the soul, indicating it involves true faith in God and in his righteousness, high culture, and a love for the finer things in life.
>
> True reverence is a vital quality, but one that is fast disappearing in the world as the forces of evil broaden their influences. We cannot fully comprehend the power for good we can wield if the millions of members of Christ's true church will serve as models of reverent behavior. We cannot imagine the additional

numbers of lives we could touch. Perhaps even more important, *we cannot foresee the great spiritual impact on our own families if we become the reverent people we know we should be.* (Spencer W. Kimball, *We Should Be a Reverent People* [pamphlet, 1976], p. 4; italics added.)

What of the mother who taught her son to respect life and others? Do you think a spirit of reverence helped teach him by her good example?

A little second-grader, in the midst of snickering from his classmates, stood tall and responded to the teacher's inquiry as to who might like to be a neighbor to cross old Mr. Black, the man in the story they had just heard. The boy's mother was unaware of her teaching recorded in the heart of her child, a teaching that rippled out to everyone in the class as her son looked first at the teacher, then at the children, and said with conviction, "I wish Mr. Black was my neighbor, because if he was my neighbor, my mom would make a pie for me to take to him. Then he wouldn't be that way anymore." Another child responded, "I wish I'd said that." (Ardeth G. Kapp, *Miracles in Pinafores and Bluejeans* [Salt Lake City: Deseret Book Company, 1977], p. 18.) And a mother's labors were recorded in the "fleshy tables of the heart" of her child and others.

And what of the woman whose reverent example inspired her child? Do you think she was an example of the believers? This message was given to her in a card on Christmas morning from her daughter:

"Mother, today I decided to thank everyone for the gifts they have shared with me. I saved you for last. I could write a book on the gifts you have given me. It's only right that a mother would give the most. I could thank you for teaching me to sew, to cook, to clean house, and I do thank you for those lessons. But today, Mother, I want to thank you for the lessons you have taught that mean the very most. You know how the scripture goes—Joseph Smith has done more, save Jesus Christ, for our salvation than any man. Well, next to those two, Mother, is you! You have taught me through the Spirit that Jesus Christ lives! I could write poetry, beautiful words—but could it mean more than just this: because of your influence on my life, Jesus is a real person to me. Because of you I know he lives. In D&C 18:15–16 it says your joy will be great if you bring one soul unto Christ. Mother I hope your joy is full—because of you, mine is. Mother, I know He lives! I love Him. I love you!" (Janice M. Weinheimer, *Families Are Forever, If I Can Just Get Through Today!* [Salt Lake City: Deseret Book Company, 1979], p. 121; used by permission.)

And what of the spirit of reverence of another woman. Did she teach by an "example in spirit"? From two journal entries of Becky Smith, just eleven years old, we read:

July 15, 1978

Mark and Kevin were riding bikes when they saw two swallows swoop down so they stopped. It was a robin (less than a month old). The two parents had been killed by a cat so they buried the parents and brought the baby to me! So I am now the mother to a baby robin. We don't know if it will live since it doesn't have its true parents but I hope so!!! We got it on the 15th.

July 16, 1978

My poor little robin. It's so sick. We gave it a blessing and I'm staying home from Church. I was holding it in its little blanket when it looked up at me as if to say, "Thank you for trying to help me," and closed its dear little eyes for good. I buried it in a gold box under my rose bush. I'm very sad but where it is I know it is safe and I hope to see it in heaven. I know it is happy and that God will take care of it.

And then a final entry for that day:

My Mom and I went to the mountains to get some wild flowers. It was fun. She is a great great comforter. (Ardeth Greene Kapp, *All Kinds of Mothers* [Salt Lake City: Deseret Book Company, 1979], pp. 12–13; used by permission.)

Because of her mother's part in that happening, recorded in the heart of the child is an increased reverence for life, for birds, flowers, and mountains, and all of God's creations. Her mom, her "great great comforter," reached out to the tender feelings of her child.

The most reverent experiences I have had haven't necessarily been in the house of the Lord, although a deep spirit of reverence is to be found there.

I have felt that sacred attitude of reverence, that spirit of reverence, in many places—as I stood on the battle-grounds of the American Revolution, nestled one of my children in my arms, received counsel from a loving parent, received comfort from a tender husband, heard that which is said before a sacred altar, gave support to a beloved friend, knelt in humble prayer, faced a roomful of God's daughters, was carried away in the beauty of the earth, saw a rainbow or sunset or sunrise, felt my own insignificance, and even just sat in my own home.

Reverence comes from deep within, from remembering a sense of dignity and great, great worth. It is a quality to be sought after and developed. It is a quality that God himself possesses. It is a quality in which, to the world, we can indeed be an example. It is a quality we need to develop to become like Jesus.

Fruits of Faith

Be thou an example in faith. This past summer my family and I had the opportunity to visit Independence, Missouri, and the Church's visitors' center there. There was a slide presentation which told of the early Saints' exodus from Kirtland to Jackson County.

The Prophet Joseph Smith had told the members that the Lord had revealed to him that Zion would be built there. Faithfully, they followed him and began to build homes, farms, and businesses. They thought this was their beautiful Zion, their promised place, and that there they would have peace and be able to settle.

The persecution started shortly after their arrival and became increasingly more hostile and terrible. They were driven out of Jackson County into other areas of Missouri. Persecution developed there too. With the loss of homes, the burning, the murders, and the extermination order against the Mormons, it became apparent to the Saints that they would have to leave the state. This was enforced by the mob militia, who arrested the Prophet Joseph Smith and other Church leaders who were then confined to prison for months without being convicted of any crime.

The slide presentation pointed out the unrest among the Saints. Several of the leaders fell away, disbelieving the Prophet and his revelations. You can see how faith was tested. The Saints had thought they were settling Zion permanently according to divine revelation and instead found themselves being driven out again.

Faith is a power. Many who fell away did so because they were of "little faith" and failed to see what was really happening. The slide presentation quoted from the journal of one of the faithful women who by the Spirit and because of her great faith saw clearly what was happening. She said, in effect, "There has been a falling away by many who say Joseph isn't a prophet. But I can see that a *great sifting* is taking place. The Lord is sifting his people for something more. He wants a strong and mighty people."

How true that was and is! Looking back we can now see that is exactly what happened. He sifted out the most valiant in Missouri and led them to Nauvoo. From Nauvoo he sifted again. Those who went West were of the strongest and most faithful blood. They had to be in order to establish a religion that would someday have millions of members. Only the most faithful would go West. Faith is the power of God. He needed that power in full strength in order for his church to survive and grow strong.

After my trip to Independence, I was also privileged to get another glimpse of this *sifting* in a sacrament meeting in my home ward. A couple had just returned from Ecuador, having served faithfully as mission president and wife. They were reporting their mission and giving data on the Church in South America in general.

The man said that the growth and baptisms there are in the hundreds per month. Many are coming into the Church. He said, however, that there are also many who fall away or become dissatisfied. His specific comments were: "What we are seeing is the rise of a strong membership in South America. We are seeing a sifting. The Lord wants a strong people."

As I thought about these two separate witnesses of a sifting, it was clear to me that the Lord wants the Heber C. Kimballs, the Eliza R. Snows, the Brigham Youngs, and the Mary Fielding Smiths. He wants us and needs us, those who will be faithful and valiant to Jesus Christ *no matter what*. He wants us to be committed.

Sister Eliza R. Snow says that her father, in assisting widows and others, was detained until the very last day of grace allotted to the Mormons for leaving the county; the weather was very cold, indeed, and the ground was covered with snow. She walked on to warm her aching feet until the teams would overtake her; meanwhile she met one of the so-called militia, who abruptly accosted her: "Well, I think this will cure you of your faith." The young heroine looked him steadily in the eye and replied: "It will take more than this to cure me of my faith." His countenance fell, and he responded, "I must confess you are a better soldier than I am." (Barbara B. Smith, "Blueprints for Living," *Blueprints for Living,* vol. 1, p. 37.)

Listen to the words of Heber C. Kimball:

We think we are secure here in the chambers of the everlasting hills, where we can close those few doors of the canyons against mobs and persecutors, the wicked and the vile, who have always beset us with violence and robbery, but I want to say to you, my brethren, the time is coming when we will be mixed up in these now peaceful valleys to the extent that it will be difficult to tell the face of a Saint from the face of an enemy to the people of God. Then, brethren, look out for the great sieve, for there will be a great *sifting* time, and many will fall; for I say unto you there is a *test,* a TEST, A TEST, coming, and who will be able to stand? (Orson F. Whitney, *Life of Heber C. Kimball* [Salt Lake City: Bookcraft, 1967], p. 446; italics added.)

Our faith will be tested and tried and for that reason we have to stop thinking of faith in terms of something *to have* and rather think of it in terms of something *to do!*

Faith without works is dead. I have a friend who is a businessman. He and his wife are faithful members of the Church and have discovered faith as a principle of action.

Their business was growing and struggling. He had bought it with all its debts as well as all its promises and expectations. Many of the accounts receivable were not in and his cash flow was diminishing quickly despite the growth of the company.

Somehow they held on and struggled along. Their prayers were those for prosperity and peace in their finances. Problems mounted; prayers seemed unanswered. Then the phone call came that seemed to be the final crushing blow.

It was from their major supplier to whom they owed ten thousand dollars. This supplier said that if they didn't have their debt paid in full in thirty days, they would be out of business. This was of course true, because my friend's company could not continue without the material he purchased from this main source.

He went home, feeling horribly despondent. He and his wife knew they would lose everything. Crying, kneeling, and talking together, they decided they had more faith than where their dark thoughts were now taking them.

So they "went in" to the Lord. They recovenanted all their promises to him. They talked of more family involvement, more Christian service, more personal study, more sacrifice. They prayed for help, for answers, for relief. But that is not all. They told him that they had *faith* in him who is their God. And whatever he saw fit to inflict on them, so be it. They would be subject, and more important, obedient, to his will.

They got up from that prayer changed people and began *to live, to do,* what they had pledged. They began to see faith as something *to do,* and not so much as something to have.

The weeks passed, and they could see no way to gather that much money. They did not flinch; they continued in faith, believing that a way would be provided if it was the Lord's will. If it was not, they would be inspired with other directions.

A few days before the payment deadline, a letter came from a big corporation in the East. They wanted to buy as a tax shelter some equipment my friend owned. It was a proposal he had long forgotten about. Enclosed was a check for ten thousand dollars.

Faith is a principle of action.

We have all witnessed miracles of faith. My personal life has seen faith as the power behind such miracles as healing the sick or injured, gathering finances, and receiving inspiration to solve problems in my personal life and in my work. I have known faith to be the power in helping me to accomplish some task I felt unworthy or inadequate to do. And I have known faith to be the power behind communication with God, answers to gospel questions, and much, much more.

This book is filled with ideas on how we can *do* more to increase and exercise our faith. Just as the bearing of testimony is the way to increase testimony, so is the exercising of faith the way to increase faith.

We have discussed action, love of God, obedience, submission, humility, and many other things. Another way we can increase faith is to follow the prophet, to listen and obey a prophet's voice.

There are lots of voices in the world, voices that call, "Lo here, lo there." There are voices even among us as members of the Church that murmur against or criticize the prophet. When they do that, they do it to God. He said, "Whether by mine own voice or by the voice of my servants, it is the same" (D&C 1:38).

We can show our faith in the Lord by following the prophet implicitly. There are those who would tell us that this is blind obedience.

Is it blind obedience when the student pays his tuition, reads his text assignments, attends classes, and thus qualifies for his eventual degrees? . . .

Is it blind obedience when the little child gleefully jumps from the table into the strong arms of its smiling father, or is this implicit trust in a loving father? . . .

Is it blind obedience when an afflicted one takes vile-tasting medicine prescribed by his physician or yields his own precious body to the scalpel of the surgeon or is this the obedience of faith in one in whom confidence may safely be imposed?

Is it blind obedience when the pilot guides his ship between the buoys which mark the reefs and thus keeps his vessel in deep water or is it confidence in the integrity of those who have set up protective devices?

Is it then blind obedience when we, with our limited vision, elementary knowledge, selfish desires, ulterior motives, and carnal urges, accept and follow the guidance and obey the commands of our loving Father who begot us, created a world for us, loves us, and has planned a constructive program for us, wholly without ulterior motive, whose greatest joy and glory is to "bring to pass the immortality and eternal life" of all his children?

Blind obedience it might be when no agency exists, when there is regimentation, but in all of the commands of the Lord given through his servants, there is total agency free of compulsion. (Spencer W. Kimball, *Improvement Era*, Dec. 1954, p. 898.)

Who says we have to follow blindly? We don't have to follow blindly at all. We have the Holy Ghost to bear witness to us of the divine inspiration of the prophets.

Then when the Holy Ghost does so, we need never question the authority of the living president of our church.

> We, as a people, should not treat lightly this counsel, for I will tell you in the name of the Lord—and I have watched it from the time I became a member of this Church—there is no man who undertakes to run counter to the counsel of the legally authorized leader of this people that ever prospers, and no such man ever will prosper. . . . You will find that all persons who take a stand against this counsel will never prosper.
>
> . . . When counsel comes we should not treat it lightly, no matter to what subject it pertains, for if we do it will work evil unto us. (Wilford Woodruff, in *Journal of Discourses,* 14:33.)

I have listened and been impressed as television preachers have articulated their religious views. Their language is fluent and fascinating. How beautifully they express themselves!

But in sharp contrast, when the Church President comes to the pulpit, all he has to say is "My dear brothers and sisters" and I know he is a true prophet of God.

I know we are directed by a living prophet of God. That first witness of a true prophet came to me on a cold winter day in Fort Worth, Texas, in 1954 during a Primary class. The Holy Ghost bore witness to me that Joseph Smith was a true prophet. It came in another voice that I didn't hear with my ears but with my heart.

Faith in Jesus Christ is the first principle of the gospel. We cannot grow and progress without it. Faith is something *to do* rather than something to have.

My first introduction to this idea of faith as something to do came one hot and draught-stricken summer in New England.

My father had been recently called out of his own ward boundaries to serve as president of a branch with no priesthood leadership and with mostly inactive members. He didn't even have counselors for many months. The branch covered one hundred square miles, and the members had little contact with each other. The distances discouraged them from attending meetings. There were a lot of transient situations and other problems that resulted in a struggling and ineffective branch.

One busy summer day, Dad was interrupted several times with the impression to visit an elderly couple who were not able to go to church, because of poor health. He had come to love them dearly, faithful members who had been forgotten in the dwindling activity of the branch. They were too ill to attend church, so Dad saw to it that the priests brought them the sacrament each Sunday.

That day he drove the forty-five miles to their little farm. It was dusk when he knocked on the door. He was not at all prepared for what happened next.

"Oh, President Rodriguez! Come in, we have been *expecting* you."

Dad went in—how could they have been expecting him? And yet he knew he had been impressed to come see them.

"President Rodriguez, we've been praying you would come today. We have something to give you."

Dad's eyes were still adjusting to the dark room. He knew this brother and sister only turned on the lights when it was necessary. Their $219.00 a month income afforded them no phone, no TV, no car, no luxuries, and very few necessities. But even in the darkness he could see what the elderly man held in his hands.

"We asked the Lord to send you here, because we want to pay our tithing. Here is $21.90. It isn't much, but it's a full and honest tithe."

My father was overcome. Tears choked his words. How could he take this from them when they had *nothing* to begin with? To them this was a lot of money. He struggled to keep his composure. He listened as they explained how this decision had been made. How could they take the sacrament and renew their covenants and remember the Lord's sacrifice for them if they didn't sacrifice for him? They loved the Savior and believed he would bless them. Had they not, they said, had the faith to pray the branch president to their home that very day?

Dad didn't go home right away. He walked out to the back of their "mothballed" farm and knelt down. I'm not sure what all he prayed, but it was with a very humble heart and with many tears. He asked the Lord to bless these great people.

The sun was still reflecting in the early evening sky when he finished his prayer. Looking down at the ground he became curious as to the plants that were all over this small acreage. "What is this?" he thought. He grabbed a handful of whatever it was and began to examine it. Suddenly he realized—wild blueberries! Delicious, beautiful, *expensive* blueberries!

Then his heart sank. They were hard and puny, and bitter. It would take a lot of rain to mature this crop. New England was having the worst drought in twenty years. There wasn't a chance for those berries to develop. Upon further examination he found that this couple had once been able to harvest much from this land, and much of the equipment for harvesting blueberries sat idle in an adjoining barn.

Dad went back out into that field and told the Lord that if those two old people had enough faith to give 10 percent of what little they had, then he had enough faith to pray for rain. That was Saturday.

On Sunday he prayed and fasted. On Monday he drove to the farm and prayed in the field again. On Tuesday he did the same thing. It was a bright blue sky, not a cloud in sight. On Wednesday he prayed again in the fields. The news that night said, "Hot and sunny days ahead." He reminded himself that faith is something *to do*.

Was he dreaming? Slowly he opened his eyes Thursday morning. He had wanted it to rain so much he could see even now the drops falling on the windowpane. But suddenly he realized that *was* rain and he was wide awake!

The news reported that during the night a mid-Atlantic storm had changed direction and headed straight for the New England coast.

And it rained all summer long.

Blueberries?

The branch members harvested and harvested the biggest, juiciest, most delicious wild blueberries anyone had ever eaten. This couple had enough money to live comfortably for an entire year. But that was the power of their faith from the beginning—power for action to pay their tithing and to inspire my father to pray for rain and power that contributed to the increased faith of the entire branch.

Our faith, as action, will see us through this life. It will become a principle of power in our lives—power that will aid us in becoming more like the Savior and in being examples as disciples of Christ.

Fruits of Purity

Be thou an example in purity. "Some of us must wish . . . that we could be born old, and grow younger

175

and cleaner and ever simpler and more innocent, until at last, with the white souls of little children, we lay us down to eternal sleep." (Channing Pollock, "The World's Slow Stain," *Reader's Digest*, June 1960, p. 77.)

But that is not the way it is. How can we return to our Heavenly Father more pure? How can we be a better example of purity here, especially when we have to contend with so much "pollution"?

Paul said to Titus, "Unto the pure all things are pure" (Titus 1:15).

Elder Vaughn J. Featherstone tells this story of his son as an experience with the purity of the young heart.

On one of our anniversaries, I decided to take my wife out to dinner and a show. I hurried home from work, picked out a gift, placed it on the kitchen table, and said, "Now, we will go out to dinner. Let's get ready."

Our son, Scott, who was at the time about eight, said, "Dad, may I have a dollar?"

I thought here was a good chance to get the dishes done, and so I said, "Scott, if you will do the dishes, I will give you the dollar."

"All right. May I have the dollar now?"

I said, "Scott, I can't believe you said that. Usually you do the job first, and then I pay. You do the job first."

"Dad, I have to have the dollar now."

His mom, who is very understanding, said, "Give him the dollar, and if he doesn't do the dishes, you can worry about it then."

I gave him the dollar, resentfully, and he said, "Do you mind if I go to the drugstore?"

I said, "Scott, you are something else. You have a job, you have the money, and now you want to go spend it when you haven't even earned it yet."

His mother said, "No, Scott, you cannot go until after your dishes are done." I thought that would settle it. He turned and started doing the dishes. We went to the car, backed out, and started down the street. I saw a child running down the street and thought, "That kid sure looks like Scott." We got about halfway down the street, and it turned out it was Scott. I slammed on the brakes and said, "Scott, where are you going? You are going to the drugstore, aren't you?"

He burst into tears and said, "Yes."

I said, "You haven't done the job. You are going to rush down and spend that money. You aren't going to let it burn a hole in your pocket. You have to spend it first, don't you?"

His mother was kicking my leg the whole time where Scott couldn't see. She didn't want to go against my word, but she wanted to be sure I got the message, and I did. Finally she said, "Why don't you just let him alone, and then we will worry about it when we get home if he doesn't have the dishes done."

So I said, "All right."

She turned and looked at Scott, and then I gave him a stern look when she wasn't looking to be sure he got the message that I wasn't very pleased. Anyway, we went off to dinner and the movie and then came back home. I had forgotten about the whole situation. When we walked in the house, there, on the kitchen table, was a crudely wrapped gift.

I realized what had happened. I said to Merlene, "You had better unwrap the gift. I can't do it." So, she unwrapped the gift. It was a ninety-seven cent box of chocolates. He had left the price tag on it—kids don't think of things like that.

I went to Scott's bedroom and said, "I just want to tell you what a first-class dope you've got for a father. Here you were trying to be so kind and sweet to honor us—doing that work and buying us a gift. I just hope you will forgive me." I put my arms around him and gave him a big hug.

There is a purity of heart in the young that we ought to have. You see, he couldn't see that anything was wrong. All he could think about was getting the money and going to the drugstore to get a gift. Neither the dishes nor anything else was important. They would eventually get done. I was wrong to think that the only important thing was to teach him a lesson in finance and responsibility. (Vaughn J. Featherstone, *Purity of Heart* [Salt Lake City: Deseret Book Company, 1982], pp. 18–20.)

To help us become more pure in heart the Savior gave us the blueprints in the Book of Mormon, suggests Elder Featherstone in his book *Purity of Heart* (pp. 99–100).

Yea, blessed are the poor in spirit who come unto me, for theirs is the kingdom of heaven.

And again, blessed are all they that mourn, for they shall be comforted.

And blessed are the meek, for they shall inherit the earth.

And blessed are all they who do hunger and thirst after righteousness, for they shall be filled with the Holy Ghost.

And blessed are the merciful, for they shall obtain mercy.

And blessed are all the pure in heart, for they shall see God. (3 Nephi 12:3–8.)

"Blessed are the poor in spirit who come unto me, for theirs is the kingdom of heaven." The poor in spirit are those who finally realize that to follow him, to come to him, to take on his name, is their only hope for peace and salvation. The poor in spirit are those who are humble, who have a broken heart and contrite spirit. The poor in spirit have suppressed pride and self-righteousness. The poor in spirit are teachable.

"Blessed are the meek, for they shall inherit the earth." Meekness is strength turned tender. To be meek is to be strong in believing who we are and who we can become, all the time remembering to listen to the Holy Ghost as he teaches us and reveals to us our weaknesses. The meek are capable and confident people who strive with energy to improve their lives daily and who welcome correction from the Lord.

"Blessed are all they who do hunger and thirst after righteousness, for they shall be filled with the Holy Ghost." If we hunger for righteousness we will "have no more disposition to do evil, but to do good continually" (Mosiah 5:2). We will want to "stand in holy places" both with our bodies and our minds. As we do right things and seek to be in the right places, the Holy Ghost will abide with us. This companionship increases our "hunger and thirst after righteousness" as he leads us to it.

"Blessed are the merciful, for they shall obtain mercy." Of us, it is required to forgive all men (see D&C 64:9–11). If we require of ourselves to forgive and love everyone who walks the earth, we too can obtain mercy. We can also feel the peace that love and forgiveness for others brings. The pure in heart are loving and forgiving.

I have a good friend who loves music and is an accomplished pianist. She is not well known or famous for her piano playing; she is accomplished because she loves "to hear from the Lord" through music.

She shared with me a spiritual moment she had while playing the hymn "More Holiness Give Me." She (and I repeat her insight with permission) suddenly saw the hymn as a two-part message. The first sentence asks "What do you want?" The second sentence tells how this desire can be attained.

What do you want?
"More holiness give me."
How?
"More strivings within."
What do you want?
"More patience in suff'ring."
How?
"More sorrow for sin."
What?
"More faith in my Savior."
How?
"More sense of his care."
What?
"More joy in his service."
How?
"More purpose in prayer."
What?
"More gratitude give me."
How?
"More trust in the Lord."
What?
"More pride in his glory."
How?
"More hope in his word."
What?
"More tears for his sorrow."
How?
"More pain at his grief."
What?
"More meekness in trial."
How?

"More praise for relief."
What?
"More purity give me."
How?
"More strength to o'ercome."
What?
"More freedom from earthstains."
How?
"More longing for home."
What?
"More fit for the kingdom."
How?
"More used would I be."
What do you want, really want?
"More blessed and holy."
How?
"More, Savior, like thee."
(*Hymns, 1985,* no. 131.)

Bryon Buckingham said, "Make my heart transparent as pure crystal that the world, jealous of me, may see the foulest thought my heart does hold" (quoted in Featherstone, *Purity of Heart,* p. 98).

Wouldn't it be an incredible freedom to have hearts so pure that we wouldn't mind who looked into them? We wouldn't mind if we wore hearts transparent as crystal if we had purity.

So this life rolls on. Seasons come and seasons go, and seasons even overlap. Many think that if they whine or cry or lie in bed with the sheets over their heads they somehow can halt a season, even if only for a brief time. But that's not true. The season rolls on, and if we are not striving, it rolls past us, leaving us behind.

Seasons of preparation overlap seasons of awakening, which overlap seasons of refinement, which overlap seasons of harvesting. This life was always meant to be a learning process, higher learning born of the right kind of experience. You were always meant to be, and experience, a woman for *all* seasons.

A Woman for All Seasons

A lovely woman all in white,
A burning candle in the night;
Through her study and through prayer
A time to learn and a time to prepare;
A vision easy for her to see
The woman that she longs to be.
Our loving Father, He knows the heart,
His love will set each one apart.
And with this call begins the quest,
A search to find her inner best.
For in the springtime she will find
The strength to leave her fears behind.
Darkening clouds like shattered dreams
May dim the light, or so it seems,
But with the trial comes the power
To lift her in her darkest hour.
Seasons changing, yet she knows
Given time a woman grows.
When autumn casts its shining light
Stands a woman with hope in sight.
It moves her heart to let her know
That by a word lives can grow.
It gave her warmth so she would see
The giver's hand will lift and lead

Within each season women grow,
Within their time each will know;
To love another, to lend a hand
Is all she needs to understand.

(By Charmaine McClellan, written for this book.)

Within each season we *will* grow. Within each season we can know the potential we have to become the woman God intends for us to become. We can move ourselves closer to becoming like the Savior.

Sometimes the vision of that woman escapes us, or becomes dimmed by human tears. But that woman is there, waiting for us in the future, beckoning us to come toward her. Each season brings a strange new stretching and nourishment from the last season's growth. The winter is an unseen preparation, the season of hope and promise. Spring becomes an awakening to all that we are, a season of joy. The summer is a time of refinement and the season of maturing powers. Autumn is indeed the harvest of greatness in ourselves, and of the greatness in others. Autumn has a little of all the seasons in it. It is a season of love—love for God, for ourselves, for others.

The preparation, awakening, refinement, and harvesting—as we know them—are seasons bound in "time." There will come a day when we will know these seasons in a different, higher way.

When that new day comes, when the ropes and restraints of mortality are broken, "time" will be the only thing that dies. It will be a season past. We will come face to face with a new life, with different kinds of seasons. We will come face to face with our vision of the woman we were meant to be. We will meet our Exemplar. We will no longer walk by faith, but have personal encouragement as we continue to strive to become more and more like him. We will move on into a new dimension of planting and growing. And more important, we will move to a new realm of love and personal power in a place where the purposes and fulfillments of those different kinds of seasons never end.

Then we will clearly see that we always have been, and always will be, women for all seasons.